Buried Deep in Shallow Ground

The Silent Children

By Honor Harlow

Copyright © 2021 Honor Harlow

978-1-914225-14-7

All intellectual property rights including copyright, design right and publishing rights rest with the author.

No part of this book may be copied, reproduced, stored or transmitted in any way including any written, electronic, recording, or photocopying without written permission of the author.
This is a work of fiction.

Published in Ireland by Orla Kelly Publishing.
Edited by Red Pen Edits.

For Catherine Corless and for all the children of the Mother & Baby Homes, the Industrial Schools, the motherless children taken from their grieving fathers and all the children on the island of Ireland who suffered abuse.

Acknowledgements

This book would never have come to fruition without the unwavering support from my daughter. She has been there with me on this long journey from pen to publication. Thank you from the bottom of my heart.

Prologue

When I was small, I liked going downtown holding Mammy's hand. She told me Drumbron people were proud of their town because it was special. Not every town in the West of Ireland had a giant Celtic Cross on the square, a church with beautiful stained-glass windows, a bishop's palace, nor a well-known hospital run by an order of French nuns. She said the beef factory and the railway station brought business to the town. Mammy never mentioned the Mother and Baby Home but on my first day in the big class I saw the silent children who lived in the Home. I also saw Loretta Fitzgerald whose uncle, the bishop, lived in the palace.

Loretta looked like a doll and the nun in the class treated her like she was special. Pictures of our first day in the big class are coming into my head and I am beginning to think like the little girl I was then, back when I made my First Holy Communion.

Town Map of Drumbron

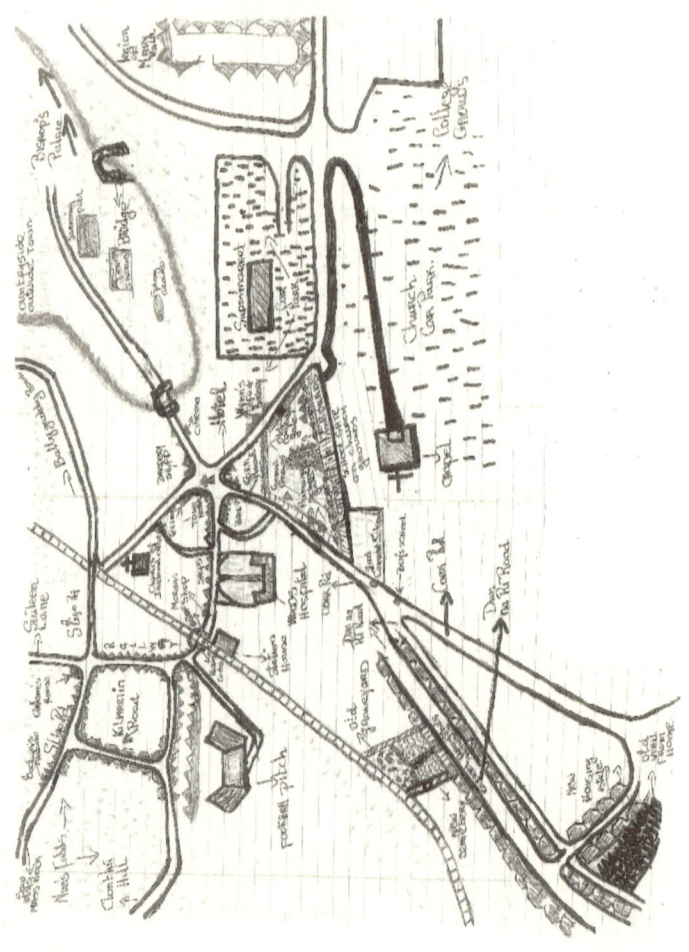

Contents

Acknowledgements iv
Prologue v
Childhood 1
Home and School 12
Mammy Always Sick 28
The Nannas on Clonthu Hill 42
Fairy Rings 51
Town 65
The Drapery Shop 76
Weekends 95
Barm Breac & The Banshee 111
The Infirmary 125
Sickness 136
Christmas 147
Lent 159
The Best Day of my Life 169
My First Holy Communion 176

Cavan 198
Storm Debbie 222
Primary School 1969 – 1972 237
Classes 263
The Boat to England 283
Glossary of Terms 292
Town Map of Drumbron 295
Coming Soon 295
Please Review 26
About the Author 297

Childhood

"Loretta, will you take the roll-book to Sister Anthony?"

"Sister Ignatius may Regina Burke come to help me?" she asked.

"Of course, my dear."

We all watched longingly as Loretta and Regina left the class. Every single day Loretta was sent out on a message for Sister Ignatius. She, and the friend she picked to go with her could skip and run along the corridor, while we had to sit as still as statues in our seats.

Loretta Fitzgerald was the *peata* of the nuns. Us other children knew we couldn't push or call her names, just like we would never push or call Sister Ignatius names. We treated Loretta the way we treated grownups, even though she was small like us. Everyone loved her, even my mammy said she looked like Shirley Temple with her head of bouncy curls. She wore beautiful shop-bought dresses, angora boleros and white ankle-socks with patent shoes.

Anyone big who came into our class always saw her and asked Sr Ignatius if that adorable, little girl was the bishop's niece. Each time the priest came into our class for catechism, he always walked down to where Loretta was sitting and spoke to her.

"Child, when I see His Grace, I must tell him what a great little niece he has."

The day the black form glided into our class and made a fuss of Loretta, we knew for sure that Loretta was special. The shape frightened everyone, even Sr Ignatius who got all jittery, twitching her shoulders and nearly tripping as she walked backwards in front of the dark thing. Loretta wasn't afraid or shaking. She smiled up at the figure, dressed in a long dress like Sr Ignatius, only the veil was a bit different because two pieces of black cloth were poking out of the sides like horns on a cow.

"Children, stand up and say good morning to the Reverend Mother."

We did as we were told, shouting out, "Good morning, Reverend Mother!" in the same sing-song tone we used when the priest visited. The stomach of the mother moved and then fingers crawled out sideways from the middle of the dark dress. They made a downwards gesture. We knew we had to sit. The big mother then floated to the desk where Loretta was, and beamed a smile from the face fenced by white and black. Our eyes widened as we watched what happened next.

"Loretta, let me see if there is any *duais* in my pocket," she said, rooting deep in a slit that swallowed her hand. As the arm disappeared into the black material, the folds in the long skirt swayed, making the giant metal crucifix and rosary beads, hanging from a leather belt around her waist, rattle. With a squeak of surprise, she produced a sweet, holding it up, so all us others could see the pink and white striped candy, smelling of cloves. She bent from on-high and offered it to the bishop's niece. As we gawped hungrily at the sweet, Loretta smiled and thanked the mother who had frightened our nun and the rest of us.

The next time the Reverend Mother came into our class, I crossed my fingers and wished with all my might she would give me a sweet. I mustn't have crossed my fingers tight enough because the treat was only for Loretta and the girls she wanted to share it with, like Regina Burke or Noeleen Pitt. In the yard at playtime, all Loretta's friends would buzz around her. She held the sugary, colourful circle on the palm of her hand, until she decided which one of her pals could suck some sweetness from it.

In our back garden, in the hot weather the bees flew around and landed on flowers, sticking their face into the centre and rubbing their thin, black arms together. Daddy told me they were gathering the pollen to make honey for the queen bee. When I saw Loretta's pals lowering their heads to lick and suck the sweet, I thought it was the flower and they were the bees. I wished I had a giant jar-jam, because I knew how to catch bees when they are twiddling on the flowers. You stand still by the flower and wait until the bee is busy rubbing its legs together. Then you slip the jar over the flower and screw on the lid on real quick before the bee can fly off.

I wanted to do the same to Loretta and her swarm. If they were locked in the glass jar, I could have the sweet for myself and lick it until my tongue was red. At home Mammy would see my mouth and think I was palsy-walsy with the bishop's niece, as she asked me the same question that she asked me every day.

"What did you and the bishop's niece do today?"

"We went to the yard and played."

"Good girl, when is she coming here to play with you?"

"One day, Mammy."

"If ye are palsy-walsy, she'll want you to go to her house."

Loretta's house was in the street near the chapel. It was a big, big house, high up to the sky where a giant could live. It had trees in the garden instead of flowers. One day in the summertime when there was no class, Mammy and me were out walking near the big, big house. The gate opened and a woman with a fox came out.

"Mammy, look! The woman has a fox around her neck."

Mammy got cross. "Sssh Mary, that is Mrs Fitzgerald, the bishop's sister."

"But Mammy, tell her the fox will bite her," I said in a panic looking up at Mammy.

"Mary, it's only a fur collar," she said, catching my hand and walking real fast so that I was dragged alongside her.

"Mammy, my legs are sore," I said pulling back to make her stop walking so quickly.

"Mary, you are such a baby. I don't know how you'll manage when you go back to school and are in the big class."

The first day of class, Mammy was sick in bed, so Daddy got me ready for school.

"Arlene, today you'll go into a different class."

"Amn't I with Sister Paul?" I asked Daddy.

"Sister Paul is in High Babies with the wee ones. You are big now, Arlene."

"Daddy, I'm not big, I'm only up to your knees," I said hugging Daddy around his legs.

He bent down and lifted me up over his head and he said, "Arlene, you are getting so tall, you'll touch the ceiling one of these days."

"Will Sr Paul come with us to the new class, Daddy?"

"No, you'll be with a nun called Sr Ignatius."

"That's a funny name, Daddy. I won't be able to say it."

"You say 'Yes Sister' or 'No Sister' until you learn how to say her name."

Daddy said I was going into first class and the new nun would teach me sums and writing. Mammy called down from her room upstairs.

"William, Mary will have Catechism too. She's making her First Communion this year."

We went to school on Daddy's bike. He came to the door of the new class and spoke for a second to the nun with the funny name. She smiled at him and then closed the door and put me in a line of children standing by the wall at the side of the room. The nun had a long book in her hands. She said it was the roll-book and we had to say '*Anseo!*' when she called our names. The first name she called was Mary Loretta Fitzgerald. A small girl, wearing a beautiful pink dress with a ribbon of white lace showing out from underneath the hem, said, "*Anseo*". The nun asked her to sit in the desk, at the front of the class near the nun's table.

Then after calling out the names of plenty more girls and boys, who sat down at the desks she pointed to, she said, "Mary Blake."

I replied, "*Anseo.*"

The girl with the lovely, pink frock, started to laugh and said, "Sister, that girl said, 'On suck!' instead of *Anseo*."

The nun looked cross and said pointing at me and then at the desk behind Mary Loretta's, "You, sit there."

I went to the wooden desk. I pushed myself into it. My legs touched a plank at the bottom, near the floor. It was for putting your feet on, but my knees hit the top part of the desk and instead of putting my feet on top of the wooden board, I pushed them under it. The curly haired girl with the short, white, fluffy cardigan turned around and stuck her tongue out at me. I stuck mine back out at her.

"Sister, that girl is making faces at me," she said.

The nun charged down. "Stand up, you bold girl."

I didn't budge because I was trying to get my feet out from under the plank. I managed to slip one out, but the other foot was still trapped underneath. A tapping sound made me look up. I saw the nun looming at my side, a vexed look on her face and a cane in her hand.

"Are you deaf? Does your mother not wash your ears?"

"My Mammy washed my ears and I'm not deaf, but my leg is stuck under the desk."

Her eyes and mouth went round and big like the time Daddy went into the sea at Trafada. Mammy told him the water was cold, but Daddy didn't care. He took off his shoes and socks and rolled his trousers up as far as his knees and ran in. He made such a funny face that we started to laugh. Mammy said, "William, no one in their right mind would go into the Atlantic in the middle of March!"

The nun's eyes were popping out of her head too, so I was laughing like Mammy did with Daddy. Her face quivered like the lid on the kettle when the water inside is starting to boil. I thought steam would come of her nose but instead she grabbed hold of the top of my cardigan, near my shoulder, and dragged me out of the desk. My foot came out of my shoe and the shoe stayed under the plank. I tried to bend down to get it. The nun pulled me towards the door. Everyone was looking at me, so I ducked my head down and let her take me where she wanted to. She flung open the door and told me to go outside into the hall until I learned a bit of manners. I was limping like Mick the Sticks, a man in town, who has only one leg.

As soon as I heard the door close, I stooped down and untied my lacers and took my shoe off. I held it by the lacers and started to move it from side to side, like the swing Daddy made for me in the garden. My Daddy showed me how to do up my shoes, so I knew I could put it back on again if I heard the door opening and the nun coming out.

When I got tired of playing swings with my shoe, I went over to the line of pegs along the wall. They were for hanging our coats up on. There was a row up high for the big people and one near my head for the small children. There were no coats hanging on the wall. I put my hands around a peg, then I lifted my legs off the floor. I was hanging on the wall like a coat. After a bit I moved one hand to the next peg and moved along from one peg to the next. It was great fun swinging along the wall. When I got to the end, I raised up one hand and grabbed the peg for the big people. Then I brought up my leg and placed it on the one for the small children's coats.

I was thinking I'd tell Daddy what a topper I was, because he was always saying I was wiry and had the makings of an athlete in me, when the door opened. Before I could jump down, the nun caught me under the arms and dumped me on the floor. While she was lowering me to the floor, she was shaking me and squeezing her hands in really hard under my oxters.

"A monkey? Is that what we have here. Well, all I can say is that a monkey would know how to behave better."

She pushed me into the classroom. All the heads of the children who were now sitting at their desks, were turned looking at the nun and me. I limped over to my desk but before I could sit down, she said, "Where are you off to, you little monkey?"

"I want my shoe."

"Loretta, would you teach this girl how to ask for things?"

"May I get my shoe, please Sr Ignatius?"

"Repeat what Mary Loretta said."

I got tongue-tied with the word Ignatius and said 'Egg-nose-uss', which made the nun cross and Mary Loretta laugh. I ducked under my desk and pulled my shoe out but when I straightened up, the nun was standing behind me. She pointed to a desk in the first row on the other side of the class.

"You sit there with the rest of the dunces," the nun said pointing to the desk at the front of the other side of the class.

I did what she told me, trying to walk without limping, knowing all the others were gawping at me.

"Hurry up. I can't be here all day watching to see if you do what you are told," the nun said. At that moment, the other door beside the big, long window full of small squares of glass opened.

A line of boys and girls came in. They had their heads bowed down like when the big people to go up to the altar to receive Baby Jesus in their mouths. They didn't have their hands joined in front of them but stuck onto their sides as though they were glued. They only moved their legs, shuffling them along the floor, making a soft rubbing sound.

They reminded me of Mr Delaney's two scrawny dogs. Mr Delaney is a friend of my Daddy's, but I don't like him because I saw him kicking the dogs with his big hobnail boots. His dogs move with their heads and shoulders falling towards the ground, and don't bark, run or jump about.

I turned around and looked at the children with their eyes looking down to the floor. When there was only a boy and a tall girl left standing, the nun said, "Úna McNulty stand up."

The girl called Úna McNulty had thick-glass glasses in a wiry frame stuck onto her nose, orange spiky hair and teeth that were too long to fit in her mouth. The nun told the toothy girl to sit in the desk behind me. I felt the desk behind shift as the girl with the carrot-hair sat down. I half turned around to look at her. The nun was pointing to where Úna McNulty had been sitting to the new girl and the boy. The girl, a long string, tall like me but narrow like a knitting-needle, and the boy, small and skinny, sat down.

The nun asked Mary Loretta to hand out the slates and the chalk to the children on the good side and told Úna McNulty to do the same on the dunce's side. When the girl with the pretty dress and shiny black shoes went up for the slates, she whispered something to the nun.

"Children, I want you to know this girl's name is Loretta, not Mary Loretta."

I wanted to stand up and said my name was Arlene, not Mary Arlene. But I did not because Mammy told me to be good and to remember children are to be seen, not heard.

The nun told us to copy down the numbers she was writing on the blackboard. Úna McNulty behind me whispered, "Move a bit. Your back is not letting me see." The nun saw her and hurried down to look at our slates. The girl with the glasses had the numbers wrong and the nun called her a dunce. My numbers were right, and the nun put me back on the good side sitting beside Loretta. I leaned over her arm and saw the first number, which is like a stick, was done right but the little duck and the wiggly one was just scribbles.

She saw me looking and said, "Sister, the chalk is heavy. My hand is tired. I didn't want to write anymore."

"Of course dear, giving out the slates has you tired. Come up here to help me." The nun got the long cane from the desk and helped Loretta move the cane down the line of numbers and told us to say – one, two, three, four, five.

After a while, she put the cane back on the desk and clapped her hands. It meant we had to make a line go into the yard and wait for our mammies and daddies. The children with no names stayed in the classroom.

Home and School

Daddy came to bring me home. I jumped up into his arms and touched the brass buttons on his uniform. He put me on the cross bar of his bike. First, he peddled slow but afterwards went real fast so we could get home to Mammy. She was up from bed and was sitting at the table. Mrs McLoughlin, the woman who comes to clean our house, had got the tea ready. Today we had boiled eggs, ham, scallions and lettuce. Daddy hit the top of my egg with the spoon and he cut the top off with the knife and put butter into the yellow part.

"Dervla, the tinker's funeral means I'll be spending the night in the barracks," Daddy told Mammy.

"Is there many of them in town, William?"

"The place is black with them which means trouble."

"Well, if you see Mick the Sweep, tell him we'll be needing the chimney swept before Christmas."

"I'll wait til the funeral is over, Dervla."

"But won't he be glad of the work?"

"He will, but I won't say anything until after the funeral."

"Why's is that?"

"There was murder at the last one. When the coffin was in the clay, one of the women started screaming they were burying a Mayo man in Galway soil."

Mammy laughed and Daddy went on imitating the way the woman spoke.

"The curse of Christ on the lock of ye. Poor auld Kate's Martin will never have a bit of peace until he's laid to rest where he belongs." Daddy left saying, "The public houses will be doing great trade tonight."

After teatime, Mammy asked me if I had made friends with Loretta Fitzgerald.

"Mammy, remember you told me children are seen but not heard."

"I did but what has that to do with Loretta."

"Well, I'm sitting in the desk behind her, and if I want to ask her to be my palsy-walsy, I'd have to talk loud over the desk. I remembered what you said about being seen, not heard."

Mammy looked down on me with a question in her eyes. I didn't want to tell her I spent the whole day on the bad side and started to talk before she could say anything else.

"Mammy, there were piles of new children in the class."

"Did you know any of them?"

"I didn't."

"What were their names? I might know their mammy and daddies."

"No Mammy, the nun didn't call out their names like the rest of us."

That made Mammy stop, and a funny look came on her face. "What were the children like, Mary?"

"They all came in together in twos."

"What door did they come in through?"

"The one that goes out to the small garden.

"What small garden?"

"The one with the statue of Our Lady inside the railings and when you open the gate, you are out on the big road."

"Mary, don't you remember I told you that is the Cork Road entrance?" Mammy said vexed because I didn't know the name of the street.

"They came in that one and not the way we go in."

The cross look was still on her face. "They are from The Home."

"What's The Home, Mammy?"

"Mary, I don't want you talking to those children. You keep away from them. Do you hear me?"

"I do but what is The Home, Mammy?"

"Well, heed me. I don't want you anywhere near those children from The Home."

Mammy never answered me when I asked her a question, so I knew she mightn't tell me what the Home was. I promised I wouldn't go near them, so she'd see I was good and then she might say something else about the children.

"I won't go near them but why have they no names. Are they like Mr Delaney's dogs?

"What do you mean?" she snapped.

"Mr Delaney's dogs have no name. He only says 'Dog' when he kicks them out of the way."

"That's enough out of you about Mr Delaney kicking dogs. God knows, he is a lovely man but unfortunate with the dogs he buys." Mammy was a silly goose to say he was a lovely man, but I didn't care what she said about him, only about the children.

"Mammy, why have the bunch of children no names."

"Because they are from The Home and have no daddies."

"I am from home Mammy and the nun calls me Mary. Why doesn't she call the children by their names?"

"Mary, curiosity killed the cat."

"I'm not a cat. Mammy, answer me why the children have no names," I said wanting to stamp my foot on the ground. I didn't cos I knew that would make her more cross, but I could not stop the puss coming on my face.

"A cheeky, bold child is what you are."

"Answer me."

"Manners Mary!" Mammy always said 'manners' when she didn't want me to talk about something, but I didn't care about manners and asked her.

"Maura McLoughlin has no daddy, and she has a name."

"What do you mean?"

"Remember we went to Maura's daddy's funeral and saw his coffin in the chapel. Maura is Maura McLoughlin.

Then, why don't the children have a name, Mammy?" Mrs McLoughlin's two girls were called Maura and Catherine.

"Mary, that's enough out of you."

That meant I have to stop talking but I didn't want to and was opening my mouth when Mammy said, in a real vexed voice, and holding her finger in front of my face. "Not another word out of you. How many times have I told you children are to be seen, not heard? But that father of yours has you spoiled rotten."

She said that daddy had me spoiled rotten in a voice that sounded like Daddy was bold. He wasn't, cos he never said 'manners', he let me talk and he answered my questions. He was always telling me, "You're the best wee lass in all Ireland, England and broad Scotland." And in the morning time he picked me up and put me on the crossbar of his bike and told me to lean against him when he pedalled to school. He was smashing and he called me lass instead of girl because Mammy said he came from Cavan and they talk different there. My nanna Arlene came from Cavan too and that is why Daddy called me Arlene. It was his mammy's name. She was in heaven. My other nanna, Mammy's mammy, was in heaven too and I had the two names Mary Arlene on me for my nannas.

After Mammy said Daddy had me spoilt rotten, she told me to eat my bread and butter and to have less talk out of me. A good long while after that, she washed me in the tin basin in front of the fire and got me ready for bed. Upstairs she helped me say my prayers and told me to go to sleep, but I stayed awake under the blankets waiting to see if Daddy would come home. When I was nearly asleep, I heard the front door open and called down, "Daddy, Daddy." He came upstairs to say goodnight and I told him about the class.

"Daddy, the nun's funny name is hard to say and the other children will laugh if I don't say it right."

"Ach, it's not a bother if you break it up."

"You can't break a name, only a plate or cup, Daddy."

He laughed and tossed my hair on the top of my head. "Look at my fingers. Now we'll say the first part with this finger – Egg. The second part with the second finger – Nay. And the last part with the last finger – Shush. It's easy now – just three small names put together."

We were laughing when Mammy called up the stairs, "William, that child has to get up for school tomorrow, let her sleep."

Daddy whispered, "Sleep tight and don't let the fleas bite."

The next morning Daddy was sitting at the table eating his porridge, but he wasn't talking. Mammy might have told him to have manners. I went to school with him on his bike and he was singing low a song about a girl called Eileen Óg and fish in the sea.

At school I was going to try to be seen but not heard so I could stay on the good side and become palsy-walsy with Loretta Fitzgerald, like Mammy wanted. When I saw the nun I said, "Sister Ignatius, may I sit where you told me to sit yesterday when you called my name from the list?"

She nodded her head and I hurried to the seat behind Loretta. She turned around to look at me and mouthed, "Monkey." Before I could stop myself, I answered, "Curly bob." Sr Ignatius saw me and told me to sit in front of Úna McNulty on the bad side. When the Home Babies filed in, Úna McNulty touched me on the shoulder and whispered, "Can you lean over a bit because your head is in the way and I can't see the board."

I looked back to nod and was able to see the Home Babies. Only one was as tall as me. It was the girl that looked like a piece of string. She had butter-coloured hair like my Daddy's. I thought it was a nicer colour than my black hair. Mammy had black hair too. Then I remembered she had told me to have nothing to do with the Home Babies, so I stopped looking at the long girl and the scrawny boy beside her.

When playtime came, Úna McNulty was behind me in the line. She asked me my name and I said, "The nun called me Mary Blake, but my Daddy calls me Arlene."

"Why does she call you Mary Blake?"

"My Daddy said there's four Marys in the class and the nun says the whole name and that way we know the Mary she wants."

"The nun is stupid not to call you Arlene. She has enough Marys without you."

"I know, I want Sister Ignatius to call me Arlene not Mary."

"That stuck-up Fitzgerald one is Mary Loretta, but the nun only calls her Loretta."

"She's special."

"I'll call you Arlene if you promise to move to one side and let me see the board when the nun writes on it," said Úna McNulty.

"I will."

"Say 'cross my heart and swear to die'."

Úna then kissed the side of her finger and then placed the finger up on her chest and then made a cross in the same place. She said I had to do the same when I made a promise. I was doing it when Loretta and her friends came near us. They started calling Úna four eyes and bottle eyes, and then ran away laughing.

"Is there something wrong with your eyes?"

"I'm short-sighted."

"What's that?"

"I don't know. Only I didn't see things in front of me in our house and bumped into them."

"What things?"

"The stool or the edge of the door."

"They're easy to see."

"For me they're not, Smart Alec."

Not being able to see a big thing like a stool surprised me but Úna didn't see the numbers on the blackboard either so our eyes might be different. "I'm not a Smart Alec."

"Alright, I won't call you it again."

"And the glasses?"

"Daddy took me to the dispensary."

"What's the dispensary?"

"A place you go to see the doctor."

"Was the doctor Dr Kelly? He comes to my house."

"I don't know. He was the doctor," Úna shrugged her shoulders. "Why does the doctor go to your house?"

"Cos he is my daddy's friend. Why does your daddy take you to the dispensary and not your mammy?"

"Cos my mammy's belly is big she can't walk fast, so she stays in the house to mind the small ones."

"My mammy is always sick in bed. Did you get the glasses in the dispensary?"

"We went to Galway."

"Why did you go to Galway for them?" I asked in wonder.

"Cos we did. The doctor told Daddy I was short-sighted and gave him a ticket for the bus and a yellow ticket for the eyes doctor in Galway.

"And what happened?"

"The doctor made me look at pictures and tell him what they were, but I couldn't see them right."

"And he gave you the glasses?"

"He didn't. It was Batt the postman who brought them in a brown envelope."

"Batt the postman comes to our house too, but he doesn't bring us glasses."

We got back in the line together after the playtime. Then during the class, we sometimes smiled at each other.

That evening at tea Mammy asked me about Loretta. I told about the lovely velvet dress with the white ribbon at the waist that Loretta was wearing and the shiny black shoes. Mammy was happy. She told me the shoes were patent leather and promised for Christmas she could make me a velvet dress on her sewing machine.

School was lovely now because in the yard, me and Úna played together. I didn't care Sister Ignatius was always calling Úna a dunce because she used to have her sums wrong.

One day Úna's father came up to the school. He told Sr Ignatius his daughter was a smart girl. She just needed to be sitting in the front and be able to see the board so she could do her sums right. After that, Sr Ignatius put Úna sitting in beside me. Some days Sr Ignatius would bring my friend with the thick glass, wire spectacles up to the front of the class and ask her questions. Although Úna answered right, the nun would say, "Is that the right answer?"

Úna stuttered "Yes."

But when the nun kept asking, "Are you sure?"

Úna would look confused and not reply.

"Answer me, you dunce."

"I don't know, Sister."

"Are you telling us you know don't the answer?"

Úna would nod her head.

"Where's the smart girl your father told us about?" or "You could be sitting out in the yard for all the good it is doing you being able to see the blackboard."

On account of the nun chastising me for being bold, me and Úna sat most of the time in the same desk in the front row on the bad side. When the bell rang for playtime, we stood up together and were in the line, one behind the other, on the way out to the yard. In the playground we played 'Tick' and other games Úna knew. The yard was divided into the good and bad side too, so we played near the toilets, while the girls Úna called 'big-shots' walked around near the windows and the door into the classroom.

One day we were playing hopscotch when Loretta and Regina Burke and the others came over to our side. They passed us, sucking a sweet, trying to *griog* us, so I said, "Stick your auld sweet up your nose, Curly Bob." and pushed against them. Loretta was a right cry-baby and went bawling to Sr Ignatius. I stiffened as I heard the flapping of the long skirt as the nun flew out of the classroom because I knew it meant I would be chastised. Sr Ignatius caught me by the shoulder and dragged me over to Loretta to apologise.

I said, "I'm sorry." with my head bent towards my shoulder, my lips pouted out, trying to look penitent. Penitent was the word Sister Ignatius used to tell us how we ought to feel when we made our First Confession. I kept the look on my face until the nun's back was turned and then I mouthed mutely, 'Tell tattler, tell tattler, buy a penny rattler, go home and tell your mother the crow bit your nose.' Loretta went galloping back to Sr Ignatius. I put on my penitent face and said, "But Sister, I said sorry. I'll say it again if you want, Sister?" but I wasn't fooling the nun. She dragged me back to the classroom.

That day was the first of the many times the nun marched me back to the classroom and made me hold out my hands. She brought the ruler down hard – three sharp slaps on each hand. She pointed to my seat on the bad side. I sat down. She stood until I composed myself into the frightened child she wanted to see. Chin hitting my chest I sat still, biting my lips, pretending I was afraid to raise my eyes, until I heard the sounds her habit made when her legs pushed against the heavy material as she moved towards the door. Once she was in the playground, I shook my red-raw hands up and down and let the tears fall down my face before I wiped them away with the cuff of my cardigan.

That was the first day but not the last I was brought in during playtime. I started thinking how I would get my own back on the bold nun. If I found the hole Alice in Wonderland had dropped into, I'd get the cake and eat it and become big. Then I would go to the convent and step on Sister Ignatius' toes and make her scream. Other times as I shook my hands to stop the pain, I'd imagine if I could drink from the bottle that made Alice small, I would run up the nun's sleeve and bite her arm.

When the whistle blew and the charging feet slowed to a trot, then to a walk and the high, shouting voices dropped to a murmur, I knew the class was making a line and coming back in, I stopped thinking about all the things I could do to make Sr Ignatius sorry for hurting me.

When the class came in, Loretta was always at the head of the line, everyone else walking behind her. She'd look at me and smirk. My eyes were brimming with tears that wanted to fall out and I was sitting on my hands because they were stinging but I didn't want her to know that. I'd half look to see what the nun was doing. If she was leaning over some child giving out to them, I'd stick my tongue out at Loretta to show her she hadn't bested me.

Loretta was a sneak, always tell-tale-tattling everything to the nun but I didn't know she also told her uncle about me calling her Curly Bob. Her uncle, the bishop, was palsy-walsy with the Reverend Mother and she told Daddy I was bold.

"Arlene, what's this about you at school?"

"Daddy, the nun said if I wasn't a Garda Síochána's daughter, I'd be in jail."

"But, lass, what did you do to make her say that?"

"Nothing, Daddy, but that auld Loretta fell, and she told Sister Ignatius I pushed her, but I didn't."

"Arlene, you know you must be a good girl when you're at school."

"Daddy, I am good. It's Loretta who's the bold one. Anyway, I don't mind going to jail. The barracks is ten times better than school and you can read me 'The Little Match Girl' from the book with the drawings."

"Ach, we'll read 'The Little Match Girl' tonight after tea, lass."

I nodded my head. He picked me up and threw me in the air, but I didn't fall to the ground. His hands were wide, and they caught me around the waist when I was coming down. I was screaming, not because I was frightened but because there was a big tickle of delight inside me and I needed to let it out. I stopped the giggly scream when Daddy said, "Arlene, people in jail only get bread and water and that wouldn't keep a tall girl like you full. Promise you'll behave yourself at school?"

My daddy was worried I'd end up in jail, so I said, "Alright, Daddy, I promise." I kissed the side of my forefinger like Úna showed me and then brought it down on my chest and made a cross there too, saying, "Kiss my heart and swear to die."

"You're a great, wee lass, Arlene."

Mammy was always in bed sick upstairs and Mrs McLoughlin came in to mind me. She told me when I was small and didn't know how to sit up on my own, Daddy used to carry me around the kitchen in his arms and tell me the names of the different things. When Mammy got better and could come downstairs, she got vexed with him.

"William, that baby was born knowing."

"Dervla, Arlene is a bright child and there is nothing wrong with that."

"Babies like Mary have to be watched."

When I was bigger and could sit up, Daddy used to lie beside me on a blanket spread on the kitchen floor and we chatted away. Mammy didn't think it was natural a baby could say so many words. She gave out to Daddy because she thought I was somewhere else before I came to our house.

"William, when that child was born, I told you it wasn't her first time around."

When I got big and could walk, Daddy used to sit me on his lap and read me stories and nursery rhymes from a big book with pictures. It was great except Mammy didn't like it. If she was sitting in the sofa or at her sewing machine, she'd tell Daddy, "William, you have the girl ruined, filling her head with nonsense about girls going through looking glasses. She has enough imagination as it is."

I didn't know why Mammy didn't like 'Alice in Wonderland'. The stories were smashing about hares with hats and rabbits with watches. They were not stupid like the one we had at school about a cat. All that cat did was sit on a mat. I told Daddy I was fed up with it.

"Daddy, in the book at school there is a cat on one page and a mat on another page. On the next page the cat is sitting on the mat. It's stupid cos the cat does nothing but sit on the mat."

"Arlene, that is the way the nun has for teaching ye how to read with the picture of a cat on the mat and underneath the words, 'The cat sat on the mat'."

"But Daddy I get fed up sitting listening to the same story every day."

Mammy wanted me to be like the cat and sit all day long without moving. She gave out to Daddy when he was showing me how to kick a ball around in the back garden. She said that was what boys do.

"William, that girl has the toes of her shoes all scuffed with you showing her how to play football. Maybe girls act like boys in Cavan but where I come from, girls are girls."

Even when I wasn't ruining my shoes kicking the ball but only playing cards at the kitchen table, she still spoke to him like he was bold, "William, put that pack of cards away. God Almighty, whatever is wrong with you? Teaching a child to play twenty-five? Before I know it, you'll have her at your weekly card games with Dr Kelly."

"William, will you stop wrestling with Mary. Do you think it's a boy she is?"

"William, let that be the last time you take Mary to the game with you. How am I supposed to teach my daughter to behave like a nice girl if she is up at the pitch listening to the lot of ye shouting and roaring like lunatics." I went to the GAA games, boxing and everywhere with Daddy without Mammy knowing.

Mammy Always Sick

Mammy was always in bed sick and Dr Kelly was forever coming to see her. In the evening time when he called, he'd sit in the kitchen with Daddy and they talked about the game. Mrs McLoughlin would get me ready for bed before she left to go home to Maura and Catherine and a short while after Daddy would pig-back me up the stairs and help me say my prayers.

One day when I came from school, Dr Kelly was in Mammy's room and Daddy was going up and down the stairs the whole time, not talking or smiling. Mrs McLoughlin gave me my tea and got me ready for bed. Instead of going home, she stayed in our house until Maura knocked on our door and told her mother Catherine was crying because she was hungry. Mrs McLoughlin waited at the bottom of the stairs and one of the times Daddy came down, she spoke to him in a whisper saying she had to go to her house but would be back early in the morning.

After she left, I played with my doll in the kitchen. When it was getting dark, Daddy came into the kitchen and brought me up my bed. He tucked me in, but he didn't help me say my prayers. After Daddy kissed me on the forehead, I pretended to fall asleep and he went back downstairs to where Dr Kelly was. I waited a few seconds and crept out of bed. I opened the door and peeked over the banister. The two of them were talking low. I heard odd words like hospitals and good hands. Then Daddy took his bike from under the stairs and pushed it out the door, saying he'd call Galway from the barracks.

I tiptoed across the hall to the window that looks out on to the garden and waited for Daddy to come back. I was looking out the upstairs front window, but my eyes kept closing. I must have fallen asleep sitting on the windowsill because my head jerked up when I heard the swish of the tires. Daddy was pedalling hard. He threw the bike against the gable end and rushed into the house. I went into my room.

When I was nearly asleep again, I heard the sound of a car outside our house. I ran to the window and saw the white ambulance. They carried Mammy out on a stretcher and put her in the back. I ran down the stairs, but Daddy caught hold of me and wouldn't let me out the door even when I kicked and screamed, shouting, "Mammy, Mammy!"

"Arlene, be still. Have a bit of wit and stop screaming. Be a good girl so Mammy gets better."

I put my head into Daddy's shoulder and sobbed with my fist in my mouth so he wouldn't hear me. I must have fallen asleep in his arms because I woke up the next morning in Mammy and Daddy's bed. Mammy was gone.

I was going to be a good girl and Mammy would come home again to us. I was going to be a good girl to stop Daddy worrying about me going to jail. I was going to be a good girl to stop Mammy giving out to Daddy.

Mrs McLoughlin got me up. I went to school half asleep on Daddy's bike thinking of Mammy in the ambulance. Daddy told me to wait for him inside the gate of the small garden behind the wall and railings.

"Mammy told me it's called Cork Road, Daddy," I said.

In the class, I sat still without budging beside Loretta and pushed my fists into my eyes when I wanted to cry. In the yard, I told Úna my mammy was sick, and the ambulance took her away.

"Arlene, your mammy will come back with a new baby."

"She won't. Daddy found me under a head of cabbage in the back garden and there are no cabbages in the garden now."

"She will because one time the ambulance came for my mammy and she came home with a new baby."

I was hoping it was true. Everyone in my class had brothers and sisters and I had none.

After school I was going to ask Daddy if Mammy would find a baby in Galway and bring it home to us. He wasn't outside on Cork Road so and I knelt in front of the statue of Our Lady in the small garden and joined my hands like the big people do at Mass. I asked the statue to make Mammy better so she could come home. I was after blessing myself and about to stand up when Daddy came along on his bike. He was smiling and told me Mammy would be home on Friday. Mrs McLoughlin was going to make dinner for us and clean the house so Mammy could rest when she got out of hospital.

While he was picking me up to put me on the handlebars, his face changed. I looked where he was looking and saw the Home Babies coming out through their door. Dad's eyes were looking at the string of a girl and the boy with the sticking-out bones, beside her.

"Daddy, Mammy told me not to have anything to do with the Home Babies. Stop looking at them or she'll get vexed with you."

He didn't say anything. His face was cross-looking, maybe he was worried Mammy would give out to him. I pretended I was falling off the bike so he would laugh and called me a daredevil, but he didn't.

When we got home, Mrs McLoughlin had cabbage and bacon ready on plates for us. She peeled my potatoes for me, but Daddy did his own by sticking his fork into the middle of one and taking the skin off, with his knife in the other hand.

Mammy came home on Friday. Me and Daddy were good. We didn't vex her so she wouldn't go away to hospital again. At school, I was a good girl too. My bottom wanted to lift itself off the seat all the time Sr Ignatius was telling us about the cat and the mat, but I sat still and only let my legs swing back and forward under the desk. Every time Sr Ignatius turned her back to write on the blackboard I waved over to Úna.

At sums time, we put a two and another two underneath the first two and then put a cross at the side of them and then drew a line and wrote the answer underneath it. It was always four, so I don't know why Loretta didn't know the answer and had to copy me. She gripped the chalk tight and took ages to write down the twos and cross at the side. The two were like ducks so they were easy to draw but I didn't tell her cos she wasn't my friend. The nun knew Loretta took a long, long time and didn't come to look at our sums until Loretta was finished.

I passed the time making my chalk squeak as I scribbled on the slate and imaged it was a mouse. When I pressed hard on the chalk, it made a cracking sound. When the nun didn't come for a long time, I rubbed the side of the chalk up and down the black slate until it was white. Then I shook it off and piles of white power fell on the desk. I pushed it together into a heap and then spread it out and pushed my finger through it and make a rabbit's face or the watch from Alice in Wonderland. When I saw the nun coming, I wiped it out with my sleeve.

The Catechism class was good at the beginning because the nun told us we would hear about mysteries and sacrifices and miracles and stories about angels, but it wasn't true. All we did was learn a pile of things off by heart to tell the priest. I knew the Hail Mary, Our Father and the Act of Contrition, which was the best prayer to know. If you were bold all the time of every day of the week and said the act of contrition before you died, it saved you from spending eternity in a roasting-hot fire in hell.

The nun told us on the altar at Mass, the priest changed bread into flesh and blood. I never knew Mammy swallowed blood when she went up to the railing, knelt down and opened her mouth for the priest to put Baby Jesus into it. So, I asked her.

"Mammy, why is your mouth not red if the priest gives you the blood of Christ? Do you swallow it before you come down to our seat?"

"Mary, God is in the Communion Host that the priest puts on my tongue."

"I know Mammy. Sr Ignatius said a miracle happened. The bread is converted into the body and blood of Christ, but I want to know if you swallow the blood."

"Mary, there is no blood, just the Host."

Mammy kept on saying the same thing and not answering my question right.

At school, every day the nun told us Holy Communion was a sacrament and a mystery, but nothing about why we didn't see blood. If I was good and answered her questions, she might tell me. The next time she asked us about how many sacraments there are I put up my hand, but she asked Loretta instead of me.

"Loretta, can you tell the class how many sacraments there are?"

"Three, sister."

"Yes Loretta, there are three and another four. Now, I want you to tell the class what the first sacrament is we receive when we are babies."

Loretta was busy counting out three fingers on one hand and laying them flat on the desk and trying to get the thumb and the first finger to stay away from the other three fingers and didn't hear Sister Ignatius.

The nun pointed to me and said, "You, what is it?"

"Baptism, Sister, when babies get christened and wear long white gowns."

"Answer how I taught you to reply when the priest asks."

"Baptism, Father."

"God give me patience! Why do we receive the sacrament of Baptism?"

"When we are baptised, our souls are cleansed of Original Sin."

"Why is it important our souls are cleansed from Original Sin?"

"So we can enter the Kingdom of Heaven."

"Who cannot enter the Kingdom of Heaven?"

"I don't know."

"You don't know because you never listen. Loretta, will you tell this stupid girl the answer."

Noeleen Pitt had counted four fingers on her hand and had put them beside Loretta's three. Regina Burke was helping them count the fingers on the two hands. She whispered seven into Loretta's ear and Loretta said smiling, "Seven, sister."

"Yes, my dear, there are seven sacraments. I know you know people who are in mortal sin can't go to Heaven."

"Yes, Sister."

"And who else cannot enter into heaven?"

"Yes, Sister."

"You know it is people who are not baptised."

"Yes, Sister."

Before the nun asked Loretta another question, I shouted out, "Are babies people too?"

"Of course they are."

"Can babies go to Heaven if they are not baptised?"

"If they do not receive the Sacrament of Baptism, their souls are not cleansed. Therefore, they cannot enter the Kingdom of Heaven."

"But babies are too small to talk or walk or to do anything bad. They are good, they don't commit sins, so why can't they go to Heaven?"

"Babies who are not baptised cannot go to Heaven because they have the stain of Original Sin on their souls."

"That's not fair."

"Mary Blake, how dare you answer like that!"

"Well, it's not fair."

"I am at the end of my tether with you. I can't have this kind of behaviour in class. Your father will hear what a bold girl you are."

"Where do the babies go when they die if they can't go to Heaven?"

"They go to a place called Limbo and where you are going this minute is to the bad side."

As she came flapping down to my desk, I rushed over to the other side, shouting, "It's not fair that babies who are not baptised don't go to heaven to where their sister is."

"Mary Blake, I have more patience than Job, but by dad, I'll see we put an end to your impertinence. I'm going to have to speak to your father about the way you are behaving."

I was shouting because I didn't want my baby brother to be on his own in Limbo.

One time when I was small and in High Babies with Sr Paul, my mammy was sick in bed. She was crying. It was dark, but I got up out of bed to go to see her and give her a kiss to make her better. I stopped at my door when I saw Daddy on the landing outside the door and Dr Kelly coming out of the room with his hands red and holding a basin. He looked at my father and I saw his mouth say, "A boy. It was a boy, Will." Daddy bent his head, and the two of them went downstairs to the kitchen. I ran into Mammy's room, but she was asleep. I came out and stooped down on the landing looking out through the banisters at the light in the kitchen. After a good long time, the doctor came out with his hands clean and Daddy had a shoebox. He gave the box to the doctor while he put on his overcoat and looked up towards where Mammy was. The doctor nodded his head and said, "Let her sleep. There's time enough to tell her. I'll be here until you come back, Will."

I crept back into my room. I heard the front door open and looked through the windowpane. I saw Daddy go out the gate. I put on my shoes and a cardigan on top of my nightdress. I sloped down the stairs and pulled the door open without making noise and went out the gate to follow Daddy.

We live a small bit out the country on Suileen Lane, where there are no houses and the front of our house is on Sligo Road, where there are plenty of houses. Daddy was on Sligo Road walking past the houses. He kept going until he got near the sawmills. There he turned down a boreen and walked as far as a big, fat, round rock with trees at the back and side of it. I stayed behind one of the trees and watched to see what he was doing.

He dug a hole in the ground with a small shovel and placed the box into it. I was going to go over to him but when his back shook, I moved away. I didn't want him to know I saw him. Everyone says boys who cry are sissies.

I wanted to ask Sr Ignatius if my brother could go to heaven, too, but she would not let me talk. As she pointed to the seat beside Úna, she said, "Mary Blake, I have more patience than Job, but by dad, I'll see we put an end to your impertinence. I'm going to speak to your father about the way you are behaving."

To show the nun I was vexed for not letting me ask, I crossed my arms and stuck my chin out with my bottom lip over my top one.

"Take that puss off you."

But I didn't because I was thinking my brother was too small to be on his own in Limbo. It wasn't fair to chastise him and put him in a different place from the baptised babies.

After a while I felt Úna brush her shoulder against mine. I looked and saw she had a marble between her thumb and finger on the part of the seat between us. I opened my eyes wide. She pushed the marble towards my hand. I took it and smiled at her. It was good of her to give me the marble, so I was going to tell her about my brother, and besides, when she was minding her small brother and baby sister near my house on Suileen Lane, she let me push the pram with the belly that nearly touched the ground. But I couldn't tell her that day because I didn't want the nun to tell Daddy I was bold and as soon as school was finished, I galloped out to the gate on Cork Road so I could tell him it was the nun who was bold. When he picked me up, I whispered in his ear the nun said the babies who were not baptised and didn't have a name didn't go to Heaven. I told him I got vexed with her and that she said I was bold.

He put me sitting on the handlebars and looked into my eyes and said, "Arlene, all babies are little angels who don't need water on their foreheads to make them good. God loves them and that is why He sometimes takes some of them to heaven." My daddy was great. I hugged him real tight. "Arlene, there's no harm in not telling Mammy what Sr Ignatius said. It's better she does not know the nun called you a bold girl. You know how she gets upset, so we won't say a word."

"Kiss my heart and swear to die if I tell her," I said. There were plenty of secrets we forgot to tell Mammy, so as not to upset her. Now her face wasn't white like milk, but she 'wasn't out of the woods yet' as Dr Kelly used to say when I was sick.

Daddy told Mrs McLoughlin to get the small room downstairs ready so Mammy could sleep in it and not have to climb the stairs. Daddy was right because after plenty of days she was walking around the house and not in bed all the time. Some days when me and Daddy pushed in the front door, we heard the clog-clog-thud of the sewing machine and saw Mammy's head bent over the black, shiny table the sewing machine was stuck in, one hand twisting the handle at the side and the other pushing the material under the gauge. Other times she was sitting near the fire, talking to Mr Delaney, a friend of Daddy's.

On account of Mammy always talking to Mr Delaney, she didn't see me when I came in from school, so lots of days I went out to play with Úna, who was always minding her baby sister and little brother in the pram.

The day after Úna gave me the marble, I told her about my brother in the shoebox, in the ground near the big, fat rock near the sawmills.

"The fat stone is the Mass Rock."

"How do you know it's called that?"

"Everyone knows it and my nanna told me people go to the spot near the Mass Rock, to bury the babies that had no names."

I was happy they were other babies with my brother because now I knew he wasn't on his own and wasn't lonely.

"Let's go there after school with the pram."

"It's far, far out the road, Úna."

"What harm and I want to see the sawmills, where my big brother gets the bag of saw-wood for the back of the fire."

"You'll get tired pushing the pram."

"Sure, amn't I always walking with the pram and besides, I'll get Kait Kenny to come and she'll push it half the way."

"I want to push the pram too."

"Only if Kait lets you." Kait Kenny was Úna's best friend but sometimes she played with me in the yard too.

On the way to the Mass Rock, two cars drove by on the Sligo Road. We were safe on the path and Úna's brother, Sheamie, got giddy and leaned out of the pram and pointed his little arm after them saying 'ar'. When we turned down the boreen, Úna told me and Kait to pick some yellow pissy-beds and daisies from the edge of the road.

"Look, Úna, it was around this spot that Daddy put my brother."

"Alright, we'll put the flowers there." And then Úna said to my brother and the other babies, "When Arlene, Kait and me are in Heaven, we'll go down to Limbo to see ye all and take ye for a walk in the pram."

Úna started humming '*Tá Goaithe an geim scathta fuar*' and Kait joined in. It was the song Úna sang to put her baby brother and sister to sleep. When they heard us singing it, they thought Úna wanted them to go to sleep and started getting cranky because they didn't want to go sleep. Úna let Sheamie, the big baby, out of the pram so he could toddle around while she showed us how to play 'King of the Castle'. She jumped up onto the Mass Rock and started shouting, "I'm the King of the castle and no one can knock me down." Kait pushed her off and stepped up on the rock and shouted the same thing until I pushed her off.

Úna was the best wee lass in all Ireland, England and broad Scotland, even if Mammy didn't tell me to be palsy-walsy with her.

On the way back home, Kait and Úna said the dump was better than the sawmills, but I didn't know cos I never went to the dump.

The Nannas on Clonthu Hill

When it was nearly time to eat plenty of eggs for breakfast and to wear something new, I told Daddy I wasn't small anymore and I wanted to walk home with my pals Úna and Kait. He asked me where they lived. I told him they lived in Dun na Rí Road.

"Arlene, that is on the other side of town, near the cemetery."

"I know Daddy, but they go from the railway station to their houses on the tracks because it is a shortcut."

"Arlene, a train could come…"

"Daddy, I won't be going on the tracks cos I don't know where they live."

"Ach…"

I didn't want him say no and told him real quick how Kait's grandmother lived on Clonthu Hill, only a small bit from the pitch that was near our road.

"Daddy, Kait Kenny goes up Clonthu Hill every day after school because she has her tea in her Nan's house."

"Does she?"

"She does and besides Úna's Nan lives near Kait's."

He smiled down at me and tossed the hair on the top of my head with his big hand and said, "My wee lass is getting big."

A good few days after the sawmills, my pals said I could go with them to see their nannas on Clonthu Hill. I was so happy that I started skipping and Kait did too, but Úna said it was more fun to play Tick. "You're 'It'," Kait shouted at her and started running, so I did too. Úna followed us as we ran past the railway station and then we galloped along the path in St Jarlath's Avenue. Úna caught Kait and then she was 'It' while me and Úna ran so she couldn't catch us.

It was great fun, and I didn't notice the houses with the gardens and the footpath were gone, until my foot hit against a stone. We were out in the country on a sandy and stony lane with cows in the fields at the sides. Úna told me the countryside was called Nuns Field and the lane was Clonthu Hill, where the nannas lived.

Úna's and Kait's nannas' houses were up at the top of the hill on the side of the lane. They were low and white and a bit shiny like Mammy's lips when she put lipstick on.

"Why are yer nanna's houses shiny?" I asked them.

Kait looked at me and said, "Why do you want to know?"

"Cos that's why." I answered but Úna was good and told me why the outside of the houses had a gloss like Mammy's lips. It was because after the wintertime, Marteen, Nanny Ward's son, and Mick the Sticks white-washed the walls with thick stuff from a bucket.

The roofs were yellow-coloured moustaches and they had small, fat, black doors.

"There's no top on the door," I said as Kait caught me and said I was 'It'.

"You silly goose, it's a half door split in the middle, so it is. Look, you lift up this latch to open the bottom part and then you put it down again to shut it. Nan likes the top part wide open except when it's lashing out of the heavens."

"Why is the door of the other house all opened?" I asked.

"For the chickens to go in and out."

I looked and saw hens around the door, their heads bobbing up and down as they pecked the ground. A woman with a wide skirt was standing in the doorway holding the bottom part of her apron in one hand and with the other one she was throwing potato skins to the hens and chickens. She did it like the priest did sprinkling holy water on Maura McLoughlin's father's coffin, saying 'Chuck, chuck, chuck' instead of prayers.

"That's Nan Gormley, Úna's nanna, so she is, and after dinnertime, Nan always gives the waste to the fowl."

"But she's saying, 'Bad ceis to ye or that' and the dog is barking, frightening the hens."

"That's Prince, her dog, and he's only barking to keep the hens from getting in front of Nan's feet, so he is."

"Why is that?"

"You want to know everything, so you do, Daddy Long Legs," Kait said looking up at my face. She was bigger than me because she was six like Úna and I was only five, but she had to look up at me because I was taller than her and Úna.

I didn't call her Squirt or Shorty because I wanted us to be palsy-walsy, like Úna was with her.

"I don't, only about nannas because I have no nanna like you and Úna."

"Everyone has a nanna."

"Mine are in heaven with Holy God."

"The two of them?" I nodded my head.

"We'll let you come with us every day, if you want." She had a different look on her face then. I smiled at her to keep her palsy.

I liked going up to the two houses with the moustache roofs. And having Prince jump and play with us. The hens and chickens were our pals too. They were always around, going in and out through the bottom part of Nan Gormley's door. She left it open so the chickens could use the kitchen as a shortcut to go out to the backyard. It was funny to see them hopping in through the front door and landing on the floor inside on their skinny legs. When Nan was sweeping the clay floor that was flattened into the ground and the chickens got in the way, she'd hold the brush with her two hands and swish it low, scattering them. The hens would squawk a 'bawck, bawck' deep from their necks. Some would run hopping on one leg while others flapped their wings and tried to fly away from the straw strands.

I took the twig that day because I wanted to swipe it like Nan did to scatter the hens. The handle was long, and I couldn't move it as quick as she did. Prince danced in front of the twig, so I put my leg over the handle and said I was a witch.

"No flying close to the light bulb now, thinking it's the moon, a girl, or you'll break it on me." There was a bulb hanging from the ceiling in Nan Gormley's house. They put the light in for her to listen to the radio she got for free because she was blind. Úna said she was the only house in Clonthu Hill with a radio, so people came to the house for the news in the evening and for the football on Sundays. They crowded into the kitchen when the weather was bad but stayed outside when it was mild and not raining.

The kitchen was nearly the whole house, except for a bit off to the side, where there was a room with a bed and a feather tick. We never went in there to lie on the bed, but we sat on the hobs when the nannas let us. The hobs were like seats at each side of the fireplace and there was a chair in front of it.

The windows were across from the fireplace on the front wall where the door was. They were small, square boxes with wide sills. Nanny had geraniums in pots outside of her windows, but Nan didn't. Inside the house, the two nannas used the sills as shelves to put things on. Nan Gormley kept her clay pipe on the windowsill near the door and had a tea canister on the other one. The statues of Our Lady and St Martin de Porras minded Nanny Ward's Woodbine cigarettes and her pension book. She kept the paraffin lamp on the other one. She used the paraffin lamp with wicks when it got dark because there was no bulb hanging from the ceiling in in Nanny Ward's house like there was in Nan Gormley's.

There was a black pump, ten times fatter than a bicycle one, stuck in the middle of a grey step on the clumpy, dried grassy patch beside the ruins of a house from the famine times. The pump had a handle at the back of its head. To get the water flowing out from the snout in the front, you had to move the handle up and down. The nannas came out with a bucket or a tin jug when they wanted water.

On the other side of the rocky road, up a small bit from the gate of Nuns Field, there were patches of weeds and bushes and clumps of tough grass that cut your fingers if you pull it. Sometimes the rocky part of the road was full of the Tinkers' wooden caravans, their long handles sliding towards the ground. The horses were loose, roaming nearby and chomping the grassy tufts. We'd see the men making camps, hammering thick, round pegs of wood into the ground. Right next to the fat stump they placed the end of a long thin rod. Then they tied the two together, by wrapping twine around them to hold them tight. Bringing the thin rod up to nearly their heads they made a round arch like the church door and then brought it down to the other side of the ground, where they tied the end to another peg. They got another bendy stick and did the same. They made the two rods meet in the middle like a humped cross. They covered it with stiff, black material. If it had pretty drawings like the caravans, instead of being black, it would be like the Queen's skirt in Alice in Wonderland. It was in front of the black tent that the Tinkers lit the fire and boiled the kettle with the water from the nannas' pump.

When the tinkers came to get the water, the nannas would stand at the door talking to them. Mick the Sweep was their favourite one for talking to, because he cleaned chimneys for people in Drumbron and had the news. He had to bend nearly double to get through the door of Nanny's cottage. She said he was a mountain of a man, but I told her he still needed a ladder for cleaning the chimney in our house.

"Indeedin he does, I see him put that wooden ladder in when he loads up the pony and cart."

"Do you see the long poles with brushes twisted around the tops?"

"Nothing gets past you, *a cailín óg*," she said wanting me to go out and play. I also knew cleaning chimneys made Mick the Sweep's fingernails have a dark stripe at the bottom. The black powder hid inside his wrinkles too, making them look like dark cracks around his eyes and his clothes gleamed like they were rubbed and brushed with shoe polish because his cap and the shoulders of his jacket were shiny with soot.

Going up to Clonthu Hill was smashing, better than going to Mass and nearly as good as going to the market with Mammy on the day there was no school. Kait's grandmother, Nanny Ward, and Úna's grandmother, Nan Gormley, were my pretend grandmothers. My own two real ones were in heaven with Holy God.

Nan and Nanny were big like the mammies but different too. Nan had hair the colour of the ashes in the fireplace and it was back from her face. Nanny's was white like a sheep's wool. They didn't wear coats, instead they had woollen blankets with fringes they draped over their shoulders and arms. When it rained, they wrapped the shawls around their heads, throwing the pointed peak over their shoulders. Their long, black skirts were puffed out by a pile of petticoats that swayed when they walked like the boats I saw in Sligo.

They had their habits for when they were dead, under the bed, wrapped in brown shop-paper and tied with a string. Sometimes they'd pull out the parcel, open it up and show us the brown dresses they were going to be laid out in. Nanny's was a chocolaty brown with a light colour square like a scapular on the chest. She was very pleased with her dress and would say, "Won't I be the fine-looking corpse with this on me?"

Nan Gormley had coins in a cloth pouch, with a string like shoe lacers, around her neck. It fell between her diddies. If it was pouring out of the heavens and we couldn't go out to play, she would let us see the money. She took the bageen off her neck and emptied out the coins into the palm of one hand and then turned her hand over the table and they would fall on to it. Our job was to make piles with the different size coins. We placed all the half crowns, shillings, pennies, half-pences and farthings into different round-towers on the table.

"Nan, what's the money for?"

"The wake! I'll have no one saying my wake was a mean affair."

"Is the money for the people who come?"

"God bless your innocence, a girleen. It's to buy the whiskey and stout, pipes and bacca."

"Will there be no sweets or biscuits for us?" Kait asked.

"*A mhuirnín*, there be any amount of sweet cake and brown bread and butter, as well as the other stuff."

"Last year Mammy let me stay up late at her uncle's wake and they sang, and Jock Connor played the accordion," Kait told us.

"Musha, there'll be no lack of music at my wake either. Sure, if I knew the priest would bury me, I'd have the keeners in too."

"Will the priest not let the keeners in Nan?" Úna asked her nanna.

"Indeedin he won't, sure isn't the bishop dead set against them all together. In the old days, before the Big Hunger, every wake had the keeners around the coffin giving the dead person a right send-off, but that was *fadó, fadó*."

As the rain lashed against the windows, we were cosy listening to the nannas telling us stories about long ago and about the fairies in Nuns Field.

Fairy Rings

One day Úna, Kait and me were going into Nuns Field to pick blackberries and gooseberries for Nanny to make jam.

"*A cailín dubh*, go nowhere near the fairy ring."

"What's a fairy ring?"

"It's soon you'll see one when you go into that field. Climb up the gate and I'll show you."

"Alright."

"Look at the circle of stones."

"I am looking."

"Keep well away from them. On your life, don't step over the stones and go inside."

"Why not? I won't fall cos I'm big."

"The Good People live inside."

"The Good People?" I said surprised anyone would live in a field with no house. "Who are they, Nanny?"

"The *sibhe*, the fairies."

"The fairies! I promise I won't go traipsing around the Good People's place," I said as I kissed my fingers and brought it down to my chest.

"*Mhaith an cailín*, respect their sacred places."

"What would happen if I did, Nanny?"

"They'll take your soul."

"What would they want my soul for?"

"They want you hollow inside, so you don't remember."

"Remember what, Nanny?"

"Their world."

"I don't care about their world, Nanny. I want to stay with my own mammy and daddy in our house."

"Ah a girleen, when you see their world and hear their singing, you'd forget everything and want to stay with them."

"I want to only be in my own house. But the fairies are mean if they don't let people stay in their world."

"It's their world and they only let the ones they want to stay."

"Who do they let stay?"

"A handsome lad or a beautiful girl when one of the *sidhe* falls in love with them."

"Why do you call them the Good People if they let no one go into the fairy rings and they steal souls."

"In the old language they are *daoine sibhe*. They don't steal souls."

"You said they did."

"Arlene, *a grá*, they don't steal your soul, you leave it behind you."

"Why would anyone forget their soul?"

"The *sidhe* world is so beautiful, you don't want to leave it, so even if your body comes back, your soul stays."

I shouted after Úna and Kait that I'd catch up to them because I wanted to ask Nanny something.

"How do you know if someone is away with the fairies, Nanny?"

"Ah, a girleen, by that empty look in their eyes."

"Why? Is there nothing inside them?"

"*Tráth, a mhuirnín*, when the Good People take a soul, they leave the person as hollow as a sucked-out eggshell."

"Nanny, are the Home Babies away with the fairies?"

"Why do you think that, *a grá*?"

"Cos they have no *smacht* on them. My mammy is always telling me to straighten up, but they slouch along, looking at the ground. Why doesn't someone put *smacht* on them?"

"*A mhuirnín*, the nuns have the heart frightened out of the poor creatures up there in The Home."

"What poor creatures?"

"The mothers and their babies."

"The Home Babies have mammies?" I asked all surprised because Mammy told me they didn't have mammies or daddies.

"Whist with the questions. Go outside a whileen. Let me smoke me pipe without having to take it out every five minutes to answer you."

Just as I was going out, Úna and Kait were coming back with a pile of blackberries. They pushed me back into the kitchen and dumped the berries on Nanny's table. Úna's mouth was black inside from eating the berries and Kait was holding up her finger to show us the thorn stuck in it. Nanny told Úna to go over to the window and take a sewing needle from a box with threads and scissors.

Kait was making faces saying her finger was sore and didn't want anyone to touch the thorn. Nanny took no heed of her and held the finger while she lifted the skin up a bit with the needle then squeezed. Me and Úna were on each side of Nanny and we saw the thick, little brown stick pop out. It was smaller than a fairy and the two of us wanted it, but it got lost. Nanny called Kait over to sit on the hob and started fussing over her.

Úna gave me a handful of berries and stuffed another pile into her mouth. Then she rooted under the bed and pulled out a long stick and a short, fat one, with the ends pared into sharp ends, that we left in Nanny's house for playing *Buille*. She skipped out the door pulling me along with her because we were tired of seeing Nanny making a *peata* out of Kait.

Úna broke a bit off the bottom of the whitewashed walls to use as chalk. She drew a box and a half circle. She told me to stand in the half circle and to throw the short, fat stick at her. She was standing in front of the box holding the long stick in her two hands. I threw the short stick at her. She tried to hit it but kept missing, so I said I was going home.

"Wait til I call Kait and we'll all go together."

On the way down the hill, I said, "Úna, the Home Babies have no souls."

"They have souls."

"They don't have souls, Úna."

"They do, so they do," Kait said as though she knew what she was talking about, so I explained it to her.

"They don't, they are away with the fairies."

"How do you know that, Know-All?"

"Cos their eyes have the look of people who are away with the fairies and I am not a Know-All."

Then Úna, who was six and a half and minded her brother and sister and stopped them fighting, said, "The nun told us when you made your First Holy Communion, Baby Jesus goes into your soul and the Home Babies are making theirs, so they have to have souls for Baby Jesus to go into."

Me and Kait knew Úna was the boss but I still wanted her to show her the nun didn't know everything, especially about the babies with no names and I said, "She doesn't know more than my daddy. He told me all babies go to heaven."

"Your daddy is a Garda, so he knows where everyone goes but he doesn't know the Catechism off by heart like the nun does," Kait said.

"Does she know it, so the priest won't get cross?" I asked Úna.

"She has to know it to teach us and the Home Babies so we can make our First Holy Communion."

Úna was smart because she was six and a half, real old. I was only gone five and Kait was only nearly six, but she still went with Úna to the dump and got money to buy things when we were playing shop in the yard. We sat on our hunkers to play shop and used the shiny biteens of glass and delph from the dump to buy things.

"A penny worth of sweets, Mrs." Úna was the shopkeeper and she separated three pebbles and passed them over to Kait, who paid her a piece of glass. Úna examined the glass. If it was big or sparkly, she would give back a bit of delph as change but if it was normal glass, Kait got no change. They gave me glass and delph to buy sweets with, but I wanted my own money.

"I want to go to the dump the next time with ye."

"You can't come cos it's a long way and you'd be late for your tea," Kait told me cos she didn't like Úna linking me when we were together.

"I can. My daddy knows I'm big and can stay out playing on my own."

"We still can't go this evening, so we can't."

"Why not?"

"Cos it was raining yesterday, so it was."

"What's the rain got to do with going the dump?" I asked with a puss on me.

"Cos now it's all messy and smelly, so it is," Kait said.

"It's not fair, ye have great fun rooting around in the dump and finding treasures."

"It was Kait who found the fairy on a box. She always finds the best things."

"Mammy said when it was new, the fairy twirled around and music came from the box, so it did."

"Was it a real fairy?" I asked.

"No, silly goose, real fairies live in fairy rings," Úna answered.

"I know, I was just asking to see if Kait knew. Anyway, if we can't go to the dump, what will we do after school?"

"Do ye want to see the house where the Home Babies live?" Úna asked.

"I saw it already," Kait said. "We hear the babies crying and the nuns giving out to them."

"I didn't see it and I want to." I was dying to see the place where the still, silent children lived.

"If ye're going, I'm going too, so I am," Kait said.

"But you see it every day, Kait."

"But soon I won't."

"Why won't you?"

"Cos we are getting a house on Kilmartin Road."

"Why do you have to get a different house? I won't be able to see you after school," Úna said, like she was going to cry.

"Cos Mammy told the town council the crying and screaming of the babies is driving her demented and if she doesn't get a house away from the Home, she'll end up in the mad house in Ballinacora."

Úna was still looking sad, so to cheer her up I said, "Mrs McLoughlin lives in Kilmartin Road, and it's near the railway station. So, me and Kait will go up the tracks to see you some days, won't we Kait?"

"Ya, we will, so we will. And we'll see the Home Babies too."

"We can't see the babies. They will be in their cots asleep," I said.

"We will see the babies who got big, so we will and not the small ones, silly goose," Kait answered. She was right because the Home Babies in our class were the babies who got big and could walk.

When I was small in Low Babies and High Babies, I never saw Home Babies in class colouring without going outside the line, or to cutting with the small scissors.

"Úna, did you see them in High Babies?" I asked Úna cos she was big and knew everything.

"They start school in first class."

"Why did they not go to High Babies?"

"Cos we don't make our First Holy Communion in High Babies."

"And?"

"We make it in first class, that's the reason why," Úna told me.

"They have to learn about the body and blood of Christ and how to tell sins in confession to the priest, so they do."

After the yard, I got in line with Úna and Kait but went to my place on the good side beside Colette Daly. Our desk was in front of Pauline Byrne and Fionnuala McCabe. I was giddy thinking I was going to see where the Home Babies lived. In the classroom, I was able to look over at them when they came in the door on the garden side, because

Mammy was sick in bed and couldn't see me watching. They couldn't see me either because they never looked up from the floor. They shuffled along in a line, two by two. The bunch of them wore black laced up boots and made no noise with their feet as they moved to their seats and sat, heads bent, on the bad side with the dunces. Úna and Kait were on the bad side too.

I was sitting with the children of the mammies and daddies that my own mammy and daddy were palsy-walsy with. Colette Daly's daddy did houses, Pauline's daddy had a shop and Fionnuala's daddy worked in the beef factory. They were nice but I liked my pals the best. Úna waved at me and I waved back. The nun saw me. She said I didn't know how to behave myself and pointed the ruler towards the bad side. I got up and sat in beside Úna and Kait in the front row of desks. The Home Babies were behind, so I turned around to look at them, but they didn't see me because they never raised their eyes. I saw their arms were like the thin, white clay-pipe Nanny Ward smokes, inside the sleeves of their jumpers knitted in a pile of different coloured stripes.

I didn't go to The Home to see the Home Babies because Daddy and Dr Kelly were outside the gate on Cork Road. He was off duty and he was bringing me to the pitch with him. Dr Kelly spoke to Úna to tell her the ambulance came for her mammy and she was to go home straight away. Kait said she'd help Úna mind the children. I went with Daddy to the pitch, at the back of St Jarlath's Avenue, and watched Daddy teach the boys how to play football and then we went home for tea.

At teatime I told Mammy about the jumpers with the different colours and asked why they weren't the same colour. She said it was because the women didn't have enough of the same colour wool to knit a whole jumper.

"Why don't they buy enough of the same colour wool, like you do?"

"Mary, they don't buy the wool, they are given it."

"Who gives it to them?"

"The good nuns."

"Then why don't the nuns buy enough of the same colour?"

"You have my head light with so many questions."

"Answer me."

"Don't be so forward but if it will keep you quiet, I'll tell you the nuns are good enough to give the mothers their own socks when the heels are worn out."

"Mammy, I'm talking about their jumpers and not about the socks."

"Mary, less auld buck and more manners."

"Alright Mammy."

"The nuns give the mothers the socks for them to rip them out."

"And make balls with the wool!"

"Mary, will you let me talk and I'll tell you why the *geansaí* are of different colours."

"Alright."

"When the nuns' socks get too thin to darn any more, they give them as a present to the mothers, so they can rip them for the wool and knit the *geansaí*."

"Socks jumpers?"

"Real jumpers."

"With long sleeves, Mammy. I saw a boy wiping his nose on the sleeve of his *geansaí*."

"Don't go anywhere near those children."

"Why can't I go near them? Will they take my cardigan to wear?"

"Mary, how many times have I told you – children are seen, not heard." I lowered my head and she continued. "God knows what kind of diseases they have and sure their heads must be crawling with lice."

I didn't want to go near the Home Babies, without Mammy having to tell me. Some were scabby and had cold sores around their lips. Others had running noses with green, thick snot stuck on the bottom. No one ever heard them speak or saw them smile. In the yard the Home Babies stood still in a pile and didn't play. It was great fun to mock them because they never answered back.

I didn't mock the stringy girl, because she made me feel funny, like the day she had her arm around the skinny boy's shoulder. I felt a big puss coming on me inside and I wanted to cry but I didn't in case Loretta called me a cry baby, but it wasn't fair the stringy girl had someone to put her arm around, but my brother was in Limbo.

Since I learned about Limbo, I hated Catechism class. Besides, I was fed up listening to the nun saying the Host wasn't bread but the body and blood of Christ. Everyone knows a loaf is thick and you can put butter on it. Only a stupid person would think the Host, thin like paper and round like a mushroom in the grass, was bread. I sat still and when my body got giddy, I only swung my legs under the desk. When Loretta called me Giddy Goat, I pretended I didn't hear her and crossed my fingers for it to be time to make a line to go out to the yard.

In the yard, I played 'Tick' with Úna and Kait Kenny. They showed me how to play plenty of games and sometimes after school we went to see their grannies or to the dump.

"If ye are going to see your nannas today, I want to go too."

"We are. Úna wants to show Nan the bruises on her arm."

"Why?"

"To see if it's the Dead Man's Pinch."

"What's the Dead Man's Pinch?"

"Nanny said if a Dead Man comes into your room at night, he will pinch you if your arms are out."

"Did he pinch you, Úna?"

"Don't know. That's the why I want to ask Nan if this is his mark."

We forgot to ask on account of Nanny shouting at us. We were running through a bunch of beautiful red flowers growing along the road. They looked like roses without the thorns or bushes. When Úna bent down to pick one, Nanny cried out in terror.

"For the love of God, throw that flower away from you and on no account smell it."

"Why?" I asked.

"It will give you a headache."

"Why?"

"They're poipeens or poppies, the fairy flowers."

The nannas knew about everything to do with the fairies. When we went up to Nuns Field to pick mushrooms, they warned us on no account were we to touch the pointy brown ones. They were *pucaí* mushrooms. If we ate them, we'd be away with the fairies for a day and a night, but it was alright to pick up the white, round mushroom, we saw in the grass. Mushrooms were lovely to eat. Nan used to put them upside down, like a cup, with a pinch of salt, in the iron pan over the coals. They sizzled and juice came into their middle. We drank it before we ate the soft mushrooms shells.

Afterwards we all ran down the hill together, with the lovely taste from the mushrooms in our mouths and went home. I cut through Kilmartin Road over to Sligo Road and to my house on Suileen Lane. Úna and Kait walked through St Jarlath's Avenue onto Railway Terrace, past the station house and then took the short cut up the tracks to Dun Na Rí Road. The railway track was a long, winding, metal ladder lying on top of small, sharp stones packed in between the wooden rungs. When Úna and Kait came with me as far as the station, they would sneak in through a gap in the metal fence of bull-wire that was supposed to keep people from going on the railway line. I'd stand and watch them leap like hares from one wooden plank to the other along the railway track.

When I knew what the nun was telling us in class, my mind used to go on the track, and I'd be flying along before Sr Ignatius ruined it all by shouting and bringing me back to class.

"Mary Blake, sit quiet. You're as giddy as a goat."

I tightened myself up and tried not to move. I crossed my fingers and wished it was time to go home, run and play with my pals, Úna and Kait.

Town

The station was a big house where men and girls, with suitcases, waited for the train to Mullingar and Dublin. In summertime Mammy, Daddy and me went on the train to Sligo and we walked out to Trafada.

Lots of puff-puff trains, with wagons of purple lumps like big potatoes, hooted their way through the station without stopping. Mammy said they were taking the sugar beet to the factory in Tuam. When the trains were going to come whizzing along the railway tracks, a man, with a dark-blue coat and waistcoat and a round cap of the same colour, blew a whistle and waved a small flag. He closed the wooden gates, with iron bars, on the two sides of the road where we walked. People had to wait until he opened them again or cross over the bridge to get to the other side of the railway track.

I used to see children go up the iron stairs holding on to the banisters. The sides of the stairs were pretty with slanted bars that crossed over each other and made diamond shapes in the empty spaces. When the children got halfway up the steps, there was a small landing and then after that more iron steps before they got to the top, to a long hall. The hall was the bridge that passed over the railway lines to the stairs on the other side for people to go down. The children ran to the middle, kneeled down to put their faces through the diamond shape and wait for the train to come along.

The long, white trail of smoke from the train took the children's heads with it. Parts of their heads came back on their shoulders when the ribbons of cloud got ripped into small, fluffy bits. Noses or eyes or heads would appear and instead of the chug-chug noise of the wheels, it was coughs and laughs that sounded.

I wanted to do the same, but Mammy said it was dangerous. We always waited for the blue man with the whistle and flag to open the gates before we walked across the road with the railway track stuck in the middle and went up town or back to our own house.

The front of our house was in the town, but the back was in the country. Outside the front door there was footpath and a street called Sligo Road. It was a big, wide, tarred road that went back to the sawmills and then kept going for ages until it got to Sligo. Mammy was careful when we crossed over it to the other side with the footpath in front of the houses. There were more houses and gardens and sometimes a car passed by.

The back of our house was in the country. There were no other houses, only fields, trees and bushes. At the gable-end side outside our railing, there was a stony lane called Suileen Lane. From the upstairs back windows, it looked like a shaky line of grey painted in the countryside. The stone walls and metal gates along the way decorated it like the trimmings Mammy sewed on my dress hems to make them prettier. The farmers used the lane to bring the cows home to milk. Cows didn't know you have to use the toilet, so they just lifted their tails and let the number two fall on the ground. Mammy didn't like the cow dung, but I thought it looked like chocolate dropped scones, frying on the road.

Suileen Lane had no houses but when we crossed over Sligo Road, the street was called Railway Terrace. It had plenty of houses with gardens and a footpath. When Mammy and me went uptown, we walked along Railway Terrace to where the railway gates were and crossed over the railway line. After walking for only a small while, Railway Terrace changed its name to Hospital Street because the Woods Hospital was on it. There were plenty of shops on Hospital Street and when I walked with Mammy to go to *An Lár* or to Mass, I looked at the shop windows.

Úna and Kait lived in Dun na Rí Road. All the houses on the road were the very same, standing together in twos, like twins. They had dark slates heads with two small windows under the forehead for eyes and a big window underneath for the mouth. The nose was a long door with tin numbers hammered into the top part, so everyone knew which house they lived in. Some people, to be really sure, had painted around their windows and doors a different colour from the other houses. In front, the houses wore gardens of grass and flowerbeds, edged by railings. Outside the gardens and gates, there was a footpath. Across the road in front of Úna's house, there were no more houses, only the big cemetery with a big, big gate and black railings on top of a low, stone wall.

All the twin-houses had a gable end at one side. It was the side that wasn't stuck to the other house. Some people kept reeks of turf in the gable end but right against the side of the house, leaving a wide space so you could go to the back yard without knocking down the turf. The back yards were like small field and some daddies dug the black clay in them and grew potatoes, turnips, carrots, parsnips and cabbage. At the back, the doors had a round knob that you turned to go into the back-kitchen or scullery. In the small, tiny room there was a window with a big, white sink under it, where the mammies washed the potatoes for dinner. They could look out the window to see the children playing and see the cabbage growing. Kait said her mother put a half curtain across their scullery window because when she looked out it, she saw the rough, stony wall of The Home and knew well what was behind it.

I don't know if others did the same, but Úna said all her pal's mammies washed the spuds in the back kitchen and brought the pot to the kitchen, with the fireplace and hobs, and put the potatoes on the fire to boil for dinner. The kitchen was big with a big window, cut into two big pieces with a sash like a white rope at the side. You could push the top part down to open it.

The children who lived in the rows of twin-houses, except a few, like Fionnuala McCabe, were always on the bad side of the class. Nearly every single day, the nun put me on the bad side. I didn't care because I was beside my pals, Úna and Kait. They played with me in the yard and we were always planning smashing things to do after school.

One day when we stood up to form the line Úna said, "Arlene, after class were going up the tracks to see The Home."

"Great," I said. I was dying to go up the tracks to see the place where the Home Babies lived.

When school was over, we rushed outside the convent to Cork Road. We waited until we saw the Home Babies plod up the road. Then we galloped across the road, turned the corner at the bank, ran down Hospital Street, past Woods Hospital and didn't stop until we reached the station.

"Kait, show Arlene the gap we go through," Úna told Kait but I was already halfway through the broken part of the wire fence. I ran onto the track for first time and felt the metal bars under my feet. Stepping onto the wooden plank, like Úna and Kait were doing, and jumping to the next one and landing as good as them without falling off was smashing.

Flying from one plank to the next one made the inside of my body giggle, scream and feel tickly. Úna, who knew everything, said the real name for the plank was sleeper. They were ahead of me. I saw Kait stumble and fall. She put out her hand to save herself and the palm got cut with the sharp stones in between the sleeper beams.

"You'll be better before you're married," Úna said and used the inside of her dress to wipe the little drops of blood. I didn't stop. It was great fun leaping like a hare but then I heard Úna calling after me cos I didn't know the spot where we'd climb over the ditch to get into the old graveyard. She told me I passed the spot.

"Arlene, if you keep jumping along the line, you'll end up in Mullingar. Come back here to where we are."

I turned back. Úna was holding down the bottom line of a bull-wire fence with one foot and holding the top length of wire that didn't have curly spiky bits, so I could scramble in between the two strands. With hunched shoulders and bent head, I stepped sideways through the gap, hoping I wouldn't get scratched. A few ribs of my hair got caught and Kait pulled them off for me. It hurt but I didn't care because I was inside the old graveyard, the magic place my pals were always talking about. It was at the end part of the cemetery where Maura's McLoughlin's father was. Úna said no one got buried in the old cemetery now cos it was from the time when people were dying all the time, and then no one had time to buy coffins or dig graves for them.

She was right, there were no gravestones, only weeds growing everywhere. We couldn't even see the ground right and supposed we were walking near a grave when a piece of a broken, wooden cross or board was stuck in the long, hard straw grass. Some of the boards were hanging loose like the toilet doors at school. They were among the scratchy dandelions and thistle plants, heaps of earth, round like Santa Claus' belly and covered in grass and weeds, bulged up. It was a great place, and we ran through it playing hide and seek. Sometimes we jumped on a heap and sang, "I'm the king of the castle and no one can knock me down." When we heard the whistle of a train whishing past and a long, white cloud of smoke from the chimney trailed through the air, we waved at it but Kait's hand started to sting, so Úna said, "You better go home and put it under the cold tap to stop it hurting." She started skipping along the path in the middle towards the new part. We followed her.

The new cemetery was as big as the football pitch, but it had graves and headstones, instead of goal posts. People were silent when they went there instead of shouting like at the matches. In the middle there was a stony path that separates the two grassy sides filled with the headstones and crosses. We ran down this long path to the black, metal gates that were at the beginning of the cemetery. Úna lived right across from the gates and Kait lived five houses up from her. They both lived in Dun Na Rí Road, so Kait crossed over the road and ran to her house. We waited for her outside, sitting on the path. She came back with water in a jam jar in case we wanted a drink.

My pals said The Home was around the corner. We moved, bundled together. Úna led the way, her two fists hiding her mouth, her neck gone, her head on top of her shoulders. I was stuck to Kait's back, stepping on her heels, frightened she'd leave me on my own. Úna stopped and we banged into her. Without meaning to, we pushed her against a pile of scratchy, lumpy, grey bricks. We jumped back, our heads telling our feet to land without noise, in case the stone giant stirred and gobbled us up.

Still shaking we were able to see it was a huge wall, higher than the one in the convent where the nuns lived. We leaned our heads back to see over the top, but it went up into the sky. Some stones in the front were a darker colour, like rows of dirty teeth in a giant's mouth.

Frightened it would swallow us, we backed away. I was shaking so I hid behind Úna though I am taller than her. She said a bit crossly, "What's wrong with you, Arlene? We came here on account of you."

"I know, but I can't see over the wall."

"Do you see that stone with the edge sticking out?" she said pointing to one of stones that stuck out a bit from the others.

"I do. Why?"

"Climb up on it. Maybe we can push you up to the top of the wall and you can look in."

I managed to get one foot on it but there was no room for the other. "Úna, I still can't see over the wall."

The girls kept pushing my bottom with their hands and saying, "Look for somewhere for your hands."

But there was nowhere my hands could hold on, so I got down. "I want to see the babies, where are they?" I whined.

"It's full of babies. They're always screaming," Kait said.

"I want to see them," I said again but I really wanted to go home.

"When I take our new baby out in the pram, I'll let you see him."

"But he's not a Home Baby."

"No, he isn't. He lives with my mammy in our house," Úna said crossly.

Kait was saying, "We see the Home Babies every day at school, so we do."

"But they are not babies."

"They are, so they are, but they got big."

"To make their First Holy Communion?" I asked.

"Ya, like we are going to do."

"If they are going to make their First Holy Communion, why does the nun never ask them any questions about the body and blood of Christ, like she does us?"

"That's why." If Kait didn't know the reason for something, she always said 'that's why'.

"Arlene, are you getting your communion dress bought from the shop?"

"My mammy is making it on her sewing machine."

They opened their eyes wide and said, "Does your mammy have a sewing-machine?"

"She does."

"That's because your daddy is a Garda and ye have money, so ye do."

Mammy had a Singer sewing machine and she made all my dresses and skirts on it. Every evening, before I went to bed, I had a wash in a basin beside the fire. Mammy put the tin bowl on a stool with cold water and then she poured in hot water from the kettle, until it was lukewarm and didn't scald me. I stood in my shift so she could wash me. The back of my neck and behind my ears and knees were the parts she scrubbed really hard. When I was clean and dry and wearing only my knickers and vest, Mammy used to fit on the dress or skirt she was making me.

Being reminded of Mammy with the sewing, gave me the chance to leave and get away from the horrible wall with the black teeth, so I said, "I'm remembering Mammy told me to hurry home in case she needed to try my communion dress on. Will ye come back with me as far as the station?"

"I can't cos Mammy is waiting for me to take the babies for a walk."

"I'll go with you," Kait said and we ran back through the graveyards. On the tracks we walked together, and I told her about my communion dress and the drapery shop on the corner of High Street and Shop Street.

"How do you know what the streets are called?"

"Cos my mammy is teaching me the names of all the streets."

"What's it called where the town hall is?"

"That's easy. It's *An Lár* and it's not a street, it's a square."

"I know, cos it's where my mammy buys turf from the countrymen on the day we have no school."

"Mr Delaney gives us our turf."

"Look, there's the gap to get out. I'm going back home from my tea," she said and turned to run back up the tracks.

I wasn't afraid and called after her, "I'm going home too for mine. I'll tell you about my communion dress tomorrow."

The Drapery Shop

Sr Ignatius told us all communion dresses are white and Mammy bought the white material in the drapery shop that was twisted around the corner of High Street and Shop Street. It was in front of *An Lár*, the place where the giant grey cross with a round face in the middle was standing. Daddy called it a Celtic Cross. When he said it, it sounded like Seltic, but Mammy told him it was a Celtic Cross, sounding like it started with a K.

I liked the drapery shop, but I didn't like the shopman, with the fat belly, standing at the door, always looking at the people outside the shop and the ones inside. His belly was round and smooth, like a small Mass Rock and his eyes were round and bulging out. He had thick, navy-blue stripes at the sides of his body. Mammy said they were braces to keep his trousers up. I asked her if there was no belt wide enough to go around his tummy and she got cross and told me to have manners and not to say things like that. It was the man with the round ball of a tummy who had no manners. He was always staring at my mammy with his frog's eyes and standing in the doorway blocking the way, so she had to pass really close to him when she went in through the door of the shop. Maybe he thought he had seen her in the pictures in the Odeon cinema. Daddy said the first time he saw Mammy, he thought she was Liz Taylor, a famous film star and was going to ask her for her autograph.

After we passed by the fat man, we went inside and over to the high, shiny, brown boards counter. The boards, all stuck together, were higher than my head and I couldn't see over them to the man behind the counter, so I let go of Mammy's hand and went out a bit to be able to look at him. He wore a navy-blue overall coat and stood in front of flat rolls of material that were on shelves. Mammy told him she wanted material to make a communion dress and pointed to a white flat roll against the wall. The man lifted it onto the counter and spread it out. Mammy touched it and rubbed it between her thumb and finger and nodded her head. The man measured the material, then he took a scissors that was tied to the counter, by a long string, and placed it at the edge of the material nearest him. The scissors opened its jaws and cut a straight line along the cloth making a lovely sound as it cut.

As the man was folding up the cloth, Mammy was opening her handbag and taking her purse out. She counted out the money and put it in little heaps on the counter. When the shopman saw the money, he reached up and unscrewed a small can on a rope above his head and left it on the counter. It was round like a tin of peas but short like the tins of John West Salmon Daddy has for his tea.

There was a clanging sound as he let the money fall from his hand into the round box. Then he leaned up to a rope stretched across the ceiling and screwed the tin back into the lid on the cord. There were a few of these ropes, like clotheslines, high on the ceiling, with round cans instead of clothes, crossing the whole shop and going into a tiny hole in a small, wooden room, like a shed, upstairs. Mammy said the ropes were called pulleys.

When the shop assistant pulled a rope, the tin went flying across the shop to the shed and went in through the tiny window. After a minute, a bell tinkled, and the same round tin came back to the counter with the change. While my head was bent backwards looking at the tin with the money, the man in the overall coat was wrapping the material up in brown paper and tying it with twine.

Before Mammy left the shop, she went to the part in the very back where there were clothes for big people and bought a thing called a corset. I watched the canister fly into the shed holding the money and come back out again.

That evening Mammy spread the white material on the table and drew out some shapes with the thin, putty biscuit that was really chalk. The scissors made a crisp sound as she cut out the top part of the dress and two roundish shapes she said were the sleeves.

First, she tacked the pieces together and then sewed them on the machine. When she sewed the round pieces along the sides, they looked like short trousers legs and were way too wide for my arms. But when she tacked them on to the top part of the dress and put a doubled-up band at the bottom, they turned into puff sleeves.

Daddy came home and I told him Mammy had the top part of my holy communion dress nearly finished. "William, I'll finish it tomorrow. I just have to make the skirt and sew on the buttons at the back.

The next evening Mammy started doing the skirt part. It looked long and wide like a bolster case before Mammy pulled the thread she had tacked into the top. Then it became narrow at the waist and all the rest spread out wide like a bell, only not stiff but moving like a ponytail. She tacked the skirt onto the top part she called a bodice, and it was a full dress.

"Mary, slip this over your head," Mammy said. Once it was on me, she fiddled with the dress before she took it off. Then she turned it inside out and ran the needle of the sewing machine over the seams. I put it on again and Mammy said, "Stand still while I take up the hem," and handed me a pin cushion as she bent her head towards my knees.

I passed her pins which she stuck in the fold at the edge of the skirt. When she had finished putting pins in the front, I then turned around so she could do the back. She had to be very careful pulling it over my head, so the pins didn't scratch me. After she tacked it, I had to try it on again before she sewed the hem with long stitches by hand.

Daddy was reading the paper and said, "Dervla, why don't you sew that on the machine. Wouldn't it be quicker?"

"Easily known you're a man. I don't want the stiches showing on the outside so that's the reason I'm doing a backstitch on the inside of the hem." She put the iron on the fire to heat it and said, "Mary, be a good girl and put this cloth under the kitchen tap. Wet it and then wring it out in the sink."

I had done this plenty of times before and knew she would then say, "Get that blanket there and spread it over the edge of the table."

Before she had to tell me, I put a sheet on top of the blanket. Daddy was looking at me and smiling because we knew what was coming next. Mammy placed my white frock on the sheet and the wet cloth over it. We watched as she started to iron. When the hissing sound and steam came out from under the iron, as Mammy pressed it on top of the damp cloth, I jumped into Daddy's arms. It was a game we played about the dragon in the iron. Mammy didn't like Daddy 'acting the eejit' with me because she said he was filling my mind with nonsense.

When the dress was ironed, she put it on me. It was a hundred times prettier than the dresses Loretta wore.

"Mammy, this is like a miracle. You changed a white tablecloth into a princess dress."

Daddy's eyes looked like they were going to cry, and he said, "Aye, Dervla, our little girl is the most beautiful thing in the whole, wide world."

"The dress turned out better than I expected," Mammy said.

Later in the evening Daddy piggy-backed me up to my room and threw me on the bed and said he was going to eat me.

"William, don't get the child wound up or she'll never get to sleep."

Daddy helped me say my prayers, gave me a kiss and went back to the kitchen and I fell asleep dreaming of my dress.

Cold air blowing on top of my face woke me up. The room smelled of clay. I leaned my head up to see why. I wished I had not because I saw the outline of a figure near the bed. It was watching, waiting for me to sit up. The Dead Man was wanting to touch my flesh, to leave his mark on me. At least my arms were pressed in tight against my sides, but my face was outside the blankets and my head was stuck up a bit from the pillow. I lowered my neck back onto the pillow and sank my body down in the bed, afraid to move my hands to pull the bedclothes up to my chin and over my head to keep my neck and face safe from the Dead Man's pinch.

When the dark shadow leaned over me, I clenched my eyes shut and screamed. Daddy came running in. I clung to him and told him about the Dead Man. He said the cold air was only a draught and the smell of clay came from the soles of my shoes. He took to his room and put me in the bed between him and Mammy.

The next morning, I was tired and didn't want to get up. I nearly got to stay at home, but I didn't because of Mammy.

"Ach, a day at home would do her no harm, Dervla."

"William, you are spoiling that child. If you weren't so soft, we'd have less nonsense out of her," she said giving out to him. He winked at me and told me we would read 'The Ugly Duckling' after school.

I was still sleepy and in half a temper when Loretta started copying the answers of my sums. She was peeping over at my slate every chance she got and rushing up to the nun's desk before me. Sister Ignatius was praising the copy-cat, as though she was the best in the class. I stopped doing my sums and sat with my arms folded, so Loretta couldn't copy my answers anymore.

The nun said, "Mary Blake, take that puss off you and copy down what I'm writing on the board."

I didn't budge and kept the puss on me.

"Mary Blake, did you hear me? Well, heed me!"

I still didn't move so she came charging down and dragged me over to the bad side and shoved me in beside the skinny boy who was always hanging on to the stringy girl.

Once the nun was back at her desk, I was able to look at the boy and see him right. He was bony with a belly the shape of the bag of flour mammy had in the pantry. His face was floury white like the sack. He was wiping his snots with the back of his hand, his small teeth biting into the lower lip on a quivering chin with a dimple. I kept looking at the dimple because me and my daddy were the only ones I knew who had a dimple in their chins. I think he bent his body over the desk to silence the sounds of the snivelling slipping out. His back reminded me of our dinners. The matted and stringy *geansaí* looked like the cabbage we ate on Tuesdays. Mammy puts the spareribs beside the cabbage, but this lad's ribs were underneath it. His stuck-out shoulders were like the wishbone of the chicken we have on Sundays.

When Sr Ignatius told him to stop whining, his sister said something in a low voice about Liam. The nun's eyes opened wide and we all turned and gawked at the girl, with hair the colour of butter, surprised that Home Babies could speak. A stirring noise, like when the kettle on the range is singing but it's not boiling, hummed in the classroom. Bubbling through our heads were the thoughts that Home Babies could talk and had names.

"What are you saying, girl?" thundered Sister Ignatius.

In a voice that stumbled to come out, the Home girl lisped that Liam, her brother, had pains for the last days and his tummy was very sore. The nun seemed outraged by being told this. She roared at the girl to take her brother to the toilets and to stay with him. There was whispering and nudging in the class as the two, heads looking at the floor, shuffled out towards the door near the big window with squares. It was closed and the girl couldn't pull it back.

"What's wrong with you, girl, are you too stupid to even know how to open a door? Mary Blake get up and open that door. That lad needs to go to the toilet by the smell of him."

Sniggers ran around the room. I jumped up from the wooden plank seat and nearly tripped on the footrest in my hurry to get out of the desk that squeezed me in. As I stood in front of the hollow-cheeked girl, she raised her eyes without raising her head. The glance from the light blue eyes felt like a hug and a giggle tickled me inside. The *grá* came out on my face in a smile. I must have frightened her cos she dropped her eyes. I pulled the door open and stood looking at the two as they rounded the corner of the garden with the statue of Our lady, to go to the yard where the grey toilets were. The sister had her arm wrapped around Liam's bony shoulders. I wanted to be on the other side of him.

"Mary Blake, what do you think you are doing, staring like that? Sit down this minute," Sister Ignatius shouted but she didn't say anything to Loretta who was laughing about the Home Boy having the runs, saying she was sure he had scuttered himself. I crossed my fingers for the break to come so I could rush out and see what had happened to Liam and the girl.

When playtime came, Loretta was the first to stand in line. She made a bolt for the small outhouse, where the toilets were, but with my long legs, I outran her and got there first. I rushed to the toilets and saw the boy, standing in front of the wooden half-door of the cubicle, only wearing his stripy jumper of black, grey, beige and white, his spindly legs like the sticks of chalk we used in class. The sister was trying to clean his bottom and legs. She had taken his trousers and underpants off and thrown what was inside the drawers into the stone lavatory. The girl was now dragging the underwear along the trough-like sink, built into the wall of the cement outbuilding.

Loretta managed to squeeze in past me. She said she was going to tell the whole class he had done number two in his trousers and started to push the scrawny lad out of the toilets so everyone could see his knotty knees and the caked yellowy brown stuff around his bottom. I got in between them and blocked Loretta's way, keeping the little squirt in and shouted at the string girl.

"Hey you, hurry up! You know well the others will be piling in here any minute now. You don't want them mocking your brother and calling him shitty arse, do you?"

The sister used the underpants to wipe his red, sore-looking bottom. After that she picked up the trousers and pulled them over her brother's boots. She then wrung out the underpants and shoved the wet garment up under her dress.

Liam whispered, "Brigid, the nuns will be cross if I don't have my drawers on."

I saw her touch his hand and tell him she'd put the underwear on him before they went back to the Home. I thought if I had a brother or sister, I would be nice to them like Brigid was to her brother. A cold, sick and miserable Liam looking at his sister with his watery blue eyes swimming in tears reminded me of the picture of The Little Match Girl with her wishing-well eyes of sadness in the big book Daddy reads to me.

While I was looking at the two, Loretta started pushing against me, still trying to get out of the toilets. I lowered my face until it was in front of hers and said, "If you go and tell the nun about this I'll wait for you after school, you little butt, and step on you with my foot and grind you to pieces, like my Daddy does to his cigarette."

"You can't do that."

"Yes, I can. I'm bigger than you."

"I'll tell my mummy to tell my uncle."

"And I'll tell my Daddy to put you in jail cos he's a Garda."

Noeleen Pitt and three more of Loretta's pal were coming over to where we were and heard. They asked her, "Will we get Sister Ignatius and tell her Mary Blake is bullying you?"

"If ye tell the nun, I'll tell my daddy and he will lock ye all up in jail."

"He won't," Noeleen said.

"He will," Regina told her. "My Daddy says Sargent Blake is a tough sham from the North – you wouldn't want to get into a fight with. Even the tinkers are afraid of him."

Loretta was looking up at me. I think she was trying to see if I could really stand on her. I lifted my leg up in the air, like we learned in the Irish step-dancing classes and put it on her shoulder. She backed away and went off with her pals, but her head was turned back looking at me, Liam and Brigid. She didn't tell-tattle because the nun didn't come flapping over to give out to me.

Brigid led Liam by the hand to the place where the Home Babies were. I remembered 'The Ugly Duckling' and how he felt alone because the other ducks mocked him. I smiled at Brigid, but she didn't smile back. Liam's face was crumpled up and I knew his bottom would be hurting him when he sat down because my arms and back hurt me awful when I got sunburned at the beach.

One day me, Mammy and Daddy went on the train to Trafada with sandwiches and a bottle of lemonade. Daddy bought me a bucket and spade in a shop near the sea. On the beach he showed me how to make castles with the sand. Mammy took off my dress so I wouldn't dirty it and I only had on my knickers and vest and a sun cap on my head. The sun was shining yellow in the sky, it felt like a blanket making the skin lovely and cosy on my arms and back.

When I got fed up making castles I skipped down to where Daddy was. He had his trousers legs rolled up and was walking along the sand near the edge of the water where the waves were coming in. When I got near the lapping water, he splashed me. I filled my bucket with water and threw it at his legs. We were laughing and having great fun. After a good while, Mammy called us back to the spot where she was sitting on the rocks to drink lemonade from a bottle and to eat the sandwiches.

Then I played in the sand again until Mammy called me to put my dress on. The three of us crossed the road to a sweet shop. Daddy bought me a sweet, fluffy thing on a long, thin stick called Candy Floss. It disappeared on my tongue, so I stuff a pile into my mouth, but it melted away very fast too. On the way back to the station, we bought cones with lovely soft ice cream. I wanted to eat mine but after a few licks, my tummy started moving up and down, making me feel terrible. I opened my mouth and the lemonade shot up, but it tasted horrible.

Mammy touched my face and looked at my arms. She told Daddy, "William, the child was in the sun too long, she got sunburned."

Daddy picked me up and carried me to the station. On the train I vomited into Daddy's big white handkerchief. Mammy was vexed because one minute I told her I was boiling hot and wanted to take my clothes off and the next minute I was shivering with the cold.

At home, my arms and legs were red. When Mammy touched them to spread a paste of bread soda and buttermilk she made, they hurt.

"Ouch! Mammy, I'm sore." I started crying and Daddy carried me upstairs. In bed, the sheets hurt me too. "Mammy, don't let the sheets touch me. I think my skin is getting too small to fit me. It's like an elastic band pressed in against my arm."

When Daddy tucked me in, he told me to sleep with my arms outside the sheets.

The next morning when Mammy looked, she saw blisters starting to appear on the red, cracked parts of my body. I told Mammy I wanted to burst the bubbles, but she said that would make my skin worse. When she saw me rubbing my hands really fast along my shoulders, she bought me cotton gloves to wear, so I wouldn't burst the blisters. They burst on their own. Sometimes I couldn't help pressing them with my finger until a sticky water tickled out. After a small while, the burst blisters changed to scabs with crusty tops. The rest of the skin was itchy and started to peel. I scratched the red parts because the itch was driving me crazy. Mammy told me not to, but I did when she didn't see me.

That time, when I was small, I had great fun peeling the strips of my arm off, but Liam wouldn't be able to see his bottom to peel his skin off and it would be red and scalded and tight, and the itch would be driving him crazy. I wished Mammy would let him come home to our house and wash him in the lovely warm water in the tin bath in front of the fire, but she wouldn't because she didn't like the Home Babies and wouldn't put bread soda and buttermilk on his bottom either. I was going to get a Marietta biscuit in my house for Liam and bring it to school and maybe that way his bottom wouldn't hurt so much. I crossed my fingers and wished school would finish quick.

At teatime, I wanted bedtime to come quick. When I was in bed, I wanted morning time to come.

The next day I couldn't get a Marietta because Mammy kept the biscuits in the press, and she would see me. Instead, I shoved a piece of my toast up my sleeve with the butter side near the skin on my arm, so it wouldn't dirty my cardigan and vex Mammy. She was looking out the window at the rain. Big raindrops were throwing themselves against the roof of the house and making a pounding noise on the ground and the sky growled every now and then.

"It's pelting out of the heavens," Daddy said as he put his cap on and got his overcoat from the back of the kitchen door. He would hide me inside the big coat when I was on the bike and go right up to the school door with me walking up against him, so I wouldn't get wet.

At school, everyone was looking at Loretta. She had a small umbrella and wellingtons and a shiny blue coat with a hood to cover the curls on her head that were tied with white ribbons on the two sides. Noeleen and Regina were asking her to open the umbrella and then to close it again. All I wanted was to see Liam, so I was looking at the Cork Road door waiting for the Home Babies to file in. I saw Brigid but no Liam. She was shivering and drops of rain were falling down her shoulders from her hair that stuck onto her head and was grey instead of yellow. She kept her head down. I couldn't question her about her brother with my eyes.

I was sitting in my seat near Fionnuala and Pauline but I wanted to be on the bad side so I could ask Brigid about Liam. When Loretta sat down, I stuck my tongue out at her and pulled at one end of the white bow. The two long ribbons fell over her face.

She screamed, "Stop it!"

"What kind of devilment are you up to now, Mary Blake?"

Before Sister Ignatius got to me, I was up and hurrying over to the bad side.

"Your father is going to hear about this, you bold girl. And you, Úna McNulty, if I see as much as a budge out of you, you will be the sorry girl," the nun said in a squeaky voice. Úna looked surprised and stared at the nun's face, red like the steak Mammy buys for Daddy, wondering why she was getting given out to because she hadn't budged since she came in, don't mind doing anything bold.

While the nun was fixing Loretta's bow, I turned around and passed the piece of toast to Brigid. The girl's eyes opened really wide. They were blue with long, brown eyelashes. My eyelashes were black and long like hers, Úna's were sandy and Kait's were normal. Brigid was gawping, her mouth opened. I was afraid she'd say something, so I put my finger on my lips.

The sky was still falling out of the heavens. That meant the class would still go out to the yard but to the part where the bicycle shed with the galvanized roof was, and crowd into it and have great fun opening our mouths and let the drops that fell from the roof into them or rushing out and jumping in the puddles and rushing back to the shed before the nun caught us. On rainy days she didn't come to the yard, but every now and then, looked out the corridor windows to see if we were bold. The class made the line, but the nun had chastised me, so I was not let out. When the rest left the classroom I waited, sitting down, in case the stupid nun came back. I hated the silly goose for not letting me out to the yard to hold my hand out under the drainpipe to see if I could keep the water in it. If the Dead Man came to my room again, I'd tell him to pinch Sister Ignatius and leave his mark on her.

My bottom got tired sitting on the seat, so I stood up and walked around the classroom and up to nun's desk. I looked around and opened it really quick. There were three long sticks of chalk. Out of spite, I broke one in four bits. Let her think the *púca* did it. Nanny Ward told us the *púca* fairy plays tricks on people. When I heard the whistle blow, I sat down again really quick and waited for lessons to begin.

We were learning, "Bless me, Father, for I have sinned." for when we went into the confession box, and, "This is my first confession, Father." to answer the priest when he said, "How long ago since your last confession, my child?" After a hundred times of saying it, I crossed the fingers on my two hands wishing school would finish soon.

Daddy was coming to pick me up and we were going to the football pitch because Daddy trained the under-16s. They were big but not as big as him. In the pitch he always left me under the stand, where I could walk on the cement seats or run between them or watch him blow his whistle. I used to see him showing the piles of lads how to kick and punch the ball on the small field of green grass, with the two tall poles at each end. He said it was a pity that girls couldn't play Gaelic football.

"You have the makings of a great player, Arlene."

"Is it because I have long legs, Daddy?"

"That's right but a player needs to be nimble and have good eyesight and that's you."

Brigid had long legs too, so she might have the makings of a great player in her as well.

In the evening after we got home, Mrs McLoughlin had the tea ready and Mammy gave out to Daddy.

"William, the pitch is no place for Mary. It would be more in your line to be here at home."

"Ach, Dervla, if I don't go and train the lads, Drumbron hasn't a chance of winning the match against Sligo on Sunday."

After Mammy gave out to Daddy, she didn't listen to what he said because she was heading out the backdoor, like she always did in the evenings, saying, "The fowl are gone in for the night to roost." and went out the back to close the shed with the straw scattered on the ground, where the chickens lived.

Mammy liked chickens. When the winter was going away, she wrote a letter and sent it off with a postal order to buy baby chickens. After a few days, a cardboard box with tiny, yellow, fluffy chickens came on the bus from Dublin for Mammy. She'd put it on the table and open it. Chickeneens with spiky legs would jump out and run all over the table. One by one, Mammy picked them up and looked at their underneaths and a cross look came on her face. The reason she got vexed was because she wanted pullets that would grow big and be chickens and lay eggs but nearly all the chickeneens in the box were cocks.

Mammy kept the chickeneens in a drawer with a hot water bottle and a towel until they were a bit bigger. Then she put them into the henhouse and called them fowl. The fowl in the henhouse went to sleep sitting on wooden poles, up high from the ground, with their claws wrapped around the bar because they were birds and thought they were on the branch of a tree.

Weekends

Daddy was teaching me the days of the week. I knew today was Friday because we had fish. Daddy told me the fish day was Friday. After tea on fish day, Mammy always went out the back door to the henhouse and came back with a squawking cock. In the back kitchen, she'd hold the jerking chicken under her elbow and put her hands around its neck. With a quick movement, one hand turning in and the other one turning out, she'd wring its neck, with the same motion she used for wringing out the face towel she wiped my face with. When the chicken stopped moving and jerking, she tied its legs with a bit of twine and hung it up on the back door of the kitchen. Sometimes when I was bold, she would say, "I'll wring your neck if you don't stop that." and I'd be good in case she did! My legs were long, and my head would hit the floor if she put me hanging on the backdoor.

There was no school the morning after. I knew it was called Saturday cos Daddy had told me. Me and Mammy got up early on Saturday and went to the market where the country people had their asses and carts around the giant cross. On the way downtown to *An Lár*, Mammy told me the names of all the streets so I would learn them. I knew when we came out the front door of our house, we were on Sligo Road. When we crossed over the road and started walking on the footpath, we were on Railway Terrace. After we walked to the railway station and went over the railway tracks, once the gates were opened and pushed back, we were on Hospital Street. It was called that because it was the street where the hospital was. The nuns who wore white habits and had stuck-out flaps on the ear side of their veils, ran the hospital. Mammy said the nuns came from France and were called The Sisters of The Good Heart. Their hospital was in a place full of trees and everyone called the hospital 'The Woods'.

The Parish Hall came after The Woods. It was a long place with windows high up in the wall and a wide, brown door. Mammy said it was hall where Daddy went playing cards and the big people went to dance at night. The barracks with the jail, where Daddy worked, was on top of Hospital Street, but the street changed its name to Barrack Street. Beside the barracks was the bicycle shop where Daddy got his bike fixed and right next to that on the corner where you turned to go to Cork Road and to our school, there was a big bank that stretched around the corner of the two streets, so it was half on Barrack Street and half on Cork Street.

Right across the street from the big bank was the big furniture shop called Cassidy's. It went around the corner of two streets but to make sure I knew I was right, I asked Mammy.

"Is half of Cassidy's shop in Cork Street and the other half in Barrack Street?"

"Mary, Barracks Street stops at the bank. This here is *An Lár*, so Cassidy's is in *An Lár* and Cork Street."

"And what street is the hotel on, Mammy?"

"The Royal Hotel is on *An Lár*."

I didn't tell Mammy because she would be cross but when me and my pals, Úna and Kait, were downtown walking with the big pram, we saw big people sitting in the hotel with glasses in their hands.

Me and Mammy always walked on the side of the street where the hospital and the barracks and the bank were but on the other side were the shops. The first shop was Moran's, near the station and then a good bit up the path, all the shops crushed together in a bunch. I knew the names of all them. Mammy bought the newspaper and sometimes an ice-cream cone for me in Byrne's. McCabe's clothing shop was next; it sold clothes like dresses and nylon stockings. Mammy bought knickers, vests, petticoats and socks for me there. The chemist came after McCabe's. Shatter's Jewellery was next, with rings and watches and earrings in the window. Shatter's was stuck onto the town hall, a long building that had a clock high up on its wall and inside had shelves full of books because one of its rooms was the library.

Mammy said the town hall was in *An Lár*, the place with the giant stone cross. *An Lár* was the place where the country people put their asses and carts on Saturdays and had the market to sell what they had. There was plenty of room for them and the bags of potatoes and cabbage and hens, and for everyone to stand or walk around, because *An Lár* was big. It was like a spider's belly and all the streets coming out of it were the spider's legs.

Church Street, the road for going to Mass, was one of the spider's legs that came out of *An Lár* near its shoulders. It was smashing because it had Wynn's Cafe and Bakery Shop on it. Next to it was Callaghan's shoe shop. Mammy was always buying shoes in there. Me and my pals never looked at the shoe shop, but we used to look in Wynn's Café and see big people sitting at tables with tea and a bun on the table. The windows had curtains falling down on each side. I suppose it was so people couldn't see in, but we did by peeking in through the spilt where the curtains didn't meet. I didn't tell Mammy that, I only held her hand and went with her from cart to cart when we were at the market.

The market was a shop in the street. It was full of carts with cabbage, turnips, carrots and potatoes on them. Men in boots and caps stood by the carts and wheelbarrows selling to mammies or other men. They sold eggs, hens, pigs, sheep, cows and horses too. When two men spat on the inside of their hands and slapped them together, it meant an animal was sold. I liked the asses that pulled the carts, but Mammy told me not to touch them and not to stand behind them because they kicked.

"Alright Mammy," I said, not wanting Mammy to get vexed because after she got the messages, we would go over to the town hall where Jock Connor played his accordion away from the asses that might kick him.

The first time I saw Jock Connors was when I was small in Sr Paul's class. That day Mammy said, "Let's see how Jock is." She opened her purse and took a penny out and told me, "Don't lose this penny before you put it into his bag."

"I won't, Mammy, but the accordion man is smart."

"Why do you say that, Mary?"

"Cos the small bag he ties to the accordion wouldn't stay open if he didn't put the wire around about the top."

"Mary," she said 'Mary' in her cross voice, "how do you think Jock can stop playing and put the bag out every time someone gives him a penny?" and I knew she thought I was a silly goose to ask her that.

"Why does he take pennies from people?"

"It's the way he gets money."

"Mammy, I want to learn to play like him and get money in a bag." She made a vexed face at me, so I didn't say anymore and only put the penny in the bag, that was sticking out from the accordion. Some market days, another man with wooden things under his arms was standing beside the accordion man. I asked Mammy who he was, but she didn't answer, so when Mrs McLoughlin came to clean our house, I asked her. She said it was Mick the Sticks.

"Why do you call him that?"

"Because he had only one leg and uses crutches."

"Where does he live?"

"In the same lodging-house as Jock in Kilmartin Road."

Mrs McLoughlin always answered my questions and didn't get vexed like Mammy.

After Mammy got the messages, we crossed *An Lár* to Church St and went into Wynn's Bakery. We didn't go into the part that had tables and chairs, but I didn't care because Mammy always bought me a bun in the shop part.

"Mammy, will you get me a bun with pink icing?"

"Mary, children are to be seen, not heard."

She bought buns for tea and a Chester cake. It was a square slice of cake for grown-ups, with currants in the soft brown middle part and it had a white, flaky crust on top. Daddy said it was a square Christmas pudding. Sometime Mr Delaney would come to visit, and Mammy would give him tea with the Chester cake. I didn't like Mr Delaney, but he was Daddy's friend.

After we came back from town, Mrs McLoughlin had the dinner ready for us and then she went home to her own house until Monday morning. Mammy made the tea in the evening and washed up the plates before she lifted the chicken down from the back door. Mammy sat by the fire and placed the cold hen against the side of her lap, holding the hen by its yellow legs above the claws, with its head hanging down towards the floor. With quick movements of her fingers, she plucked out all the feathers until the body was pink and covered in goose pimples. Most of the feathers fell into a box. She swept up the ones on the floor and threw the lot into the fire. They sizzled and melted into the coals on the fire filling the kitchen with a funny smell.

Then she put the naked chicken over a bowl and poured scalding water on it. After that she cut off the head and scaly legs and cut a hole at the top of the pimply chest and pulled the insides out. Then she'd shove her hand up the chicken bottom and draw out more pinky-red lumps. She left the heart, liver and long tubey things on the table. Then she picked up the giblets, that sometimes she called the craw, and sliced it down the middle with a sharp knife she told me never to touch. The craw was shaped like a scone but heavy. It had sand and small stones inside and the food the hens ate.

I loved watching her slit it open and separating the skin, ridged like the galvanized roof on the henhouse, from the rest. It was the lining. She pulled it from the thick brown, red meat and threw it in the rubbish bucket. All the things from the chicken's inside were put in a small saucepan and boiled to make soup for the gravy, but she didn't make the gravy until Sunday when the chicken was roasting in the oven.

Saturday evening was the day I got my hair washed in a tin bath in front of the fire because I had to be clean for Mass the following morning. I bent my head over the basin and Mammy rubbed the soap around my head and a white foam came all over my hair. I hated it when Mammy poured a jug of water over my head and face to rinse the suds off. Afterwards, I sat in front of the fire so my hair could dry. I had long black hair like Mammy, but Mr Delaney said I needed to stop growing if I wanted to be as dainty as her. When he turned his back, I stuck my tongue out at him and thought when I got taller and got strong like Daddy, I was going to put him out in the henhouse with the chickens and let them lay an egg on his head.

Before we went to bed, Mammy made the jelly. She always cut off a bit of the look-through red square and gave it to me. It was harder and chewier than the real jelly in the bowl that we had on Sunday. My teeth and mouth moved up and down before the lump broke up and slipped down my throat. She put all the rest in a bowl and poured hot water on it to melt it. She let me stir it around with a wooden spoon until it dissolved. Then she left the bowl in the press. I went to bed thinking of the lovely red jelly I was going to have after dinner the next day. It would be a bit hard but shaky and moving when it was put on the plate beside the yellow custard.

Daddy was teaching me the days of the week and I knew the morning we went to Mass in the chapel was Sunday. The church was big up to the sky and had windows with bits of colourful glass fitted together like a jig-saw puzzle that let in coloured light.

We walked into the room where there were two big holy water fonts at each side of the big doors. Mammy always dipped her fingers into one of them and blessed herself before we went into the big room full of benches. It was where the altar with Holy God was. Mammy held me by the hand as we made our way up the top, near where the altar was. I had to sit still and not fidget because I was near the priest. At communion time, I was so near the altar rails I could see the people sticking their tongues out at the priest. Mammy said I would be able to do that after I made my First Holy Communion.

Kait and her mammy and her sisters and brothers sat in the side aisle near the confession boxes. I used to look over at her and smile.

Even though the priest said the prayers in Latin everyone knew when the Mass was over. The seats would empty. People headed out the open doors and made their way down the gravelled ground towards home. Groups of the mothers and grandmothers and aunts, wearing what they called *binógs*, but Mammy called scarves, stayed at the doors outside the church and talked. Most had black handbags stuck stiff in under their oxters.

Mammy stayed in the nice front porch with the big stone holy water fonts. The porch was outside the big, middle door but still in the chapel. There she spoke to other mammies who were hers and Daddy's friends. Úna's and Kait's mammies wore *binógs* had handbags under their oxters. They stood outside by the little side door with their friends. Little by little, the mammies drifted off until only the old women who spend all their time in the chapel were left. After all Mammy's friends were gone, she would catch me by the hand. We would go back in again but to Úna and

Kait's side of the church. It was the aisle where the confession boxes and the pictures of the stations of the cross were.

At the end of all the rows of the benches there was a big statue of Our Lady. In front of her, there was a golden table where red flames danced on top of quivering night-lights. Mammy put money in the slit, lit a candle, knelt down and looked up at Our Lady with her hands clasped against her chest, the small, white, shiny rosary beads twisting around her fingers. She always seemed sad. While Mammy was looking up at the lady with the white and blue, long dress, I'd break off some of the warm, wax curls dripping from the flat stumps of the candles and roll them into shapes.

The Sunday after the fight with Loretta, I asked Mammy for a farthing and lit a candle for Liam and Brigid.

"Who are lighting the candle for, Mary?"

I lowered my head, so she couldn't see my eyes and muttered, "It's for the Babies at school."

"The Black Babies! Aren't the nuns good to be teaching you about the children they have in the missions in Africa." At school there was a square box on the nun's table with a picture of a black baby and a slot on top where we put the pennies in. After Mammy blessed herself with the rosary beads, we'd walked home so Mammy could make the dinner.

On Sundays Mammy made a special dinner of roast chicken and potatoes and peas. The peas came from a tin, but the chicken was from the henhouse outside in the back yard. The chicken was ready on the roasting tin, waiting to be put into the oven in the range. While the chicken was roasting, Mammy made the custard for the jelly. She put milk in a saucepan to heat and then she'd put a big, heaped spoon of Bird's Custard into a cup and stirred it with cold milk. It looked easy but when I asked to do it, I couldn't move the spoon though the wet, hard power. When the milk got warm, Mammy poured the stuff in the cup into the saucepan and kept stirring it while it was heating on the range. The milk became thick and yellow. It was the custard for the jelly because on Sundays we always had jelly and custard after dinner. When the chicken was nearly done, Mammy took it out of the oven and poured some of the grease into the frying pan and mixed flour into it. Then drop by drop, she poured the soup from the giblets and made lovely gravy for the dinner.

On the Sundays when Daddy didn't have to go to the barracks after dinner, he would sit on the armchair in the sitting room and read the paper. I'd lay on the floor near Daddy's feet with my big book of stories. Mammy would say, "Mary, let your father read the paper in peace. Stop tormenting him with you wanting him to read your story book." The newspaper was as wide as the chair and when Daddy winked at me, it meant he wanted me to duck under the paper and stand against him, as he read about a silly goose called Gussy Goose. When the football match came on the radio, Mammy and me would go into the kitchen. When she was talking and smiling instead of being cross, it was great.

One day in the kitchen she started talking about 'the home place'. By her voice, I knew she didn't like that time and said it was better to forget the past. I didn't bother telling her Nanny and Nan told me stories about the banshee with the comb made of bones she used on her long, wild hair or about the Ghost of Bowers and his carriage driven by ghost horses.

I didn't even tell I went to their houses, so as not to vex her or have her give out to me. She knew Irish like Nan and Nanny, but it was only when she was very, very cross she'd say *Diabhail imhuid* or *Ba cheart é a chur soir* or something else in Irish.

"Mammy, why don't you speak like you did when you were small?"

"Mary when my family left that half-savage place where no English was spoken, my father did not want another word of Irish spoken by us."

"Mammy, we are learning to count in Irish at school. I know *haon, dó, trí.*"

At that moment Daddy was coming into the kitchen for his tea and helped me count by saying '*ceathar, cúig*' but the look on Mammy's face made us stop.

At tea, I squeezed some bread and jam into my hand and ran upstairs to put it under my pillow for Liam. In the morning times there was never sweet jam on the table, only an orange jam with skins that was called marmalade. Mammy and Daddy liked it on their toast, but I didn't, and I knew Liam wouldn't either, so that's why I kept the bread and jam under my pillow for him.

The next morning I jumped up the stairs two steps at a time to get the bread and jam I had under the pillow for Liam. It was all squashed up, so I wrapped it up in the clean hankie Mammy gave me going to school and shoved it up my sleeve.

"Mary, make sure you tell your friend Loretta you want her to come to your house."

"I will Mammy," I said.

I sat in my place on the good side beside Loretta Fitzgerald and Regina Burke, but with my head turned towards the bad side, wanting to see Liam.

Regina Burke poked me in the side, "What's wrong with you. Is your head on crooked?"

I pretended not to hear and kept watching. Sister Ignatius was opening the Cork Road Door. When the children trooped in only Brigid came in, without Liam. Her face was pale and the lids of her eyes red. She went to her place in the last row. I was dying to ask her if she was able to get Liam's underpants on, before the nuns found out she had taken them off to clean his bottom with, and if the pains in his tummy were gone. I threw my eyes a few times at Brigid, but her gaze never left the floor. I wondered if children could have a squint that keep their eyes looking downwards, like Cathal McHugh who has an eye that looks in at his nose the whole time. All the Home Babies' eyes seemed to always slant down towards the ground.

The one time Brigid looked up, her face was so sad that I nearly started to cry. Liam must still be sick with pains in his tummy and scuttering himself. Loretta saw me biting my lower lip. "Giddy Goat is eating her lips," she mocked. I didn't care.

The nun called the roll and told Loretta to give out the slates. I was busy thinking we'd soon be going out to the yard and wasn't in time to pull my hands away when Loretta let my slate fall on my fingers. I was going to hit her but saw her smiling, and knew she wanted me to lose my temper and get chastised, so I didn't. We did our sums. Loretta copied my answers and Noeleen Pitt copied hers and I didn't care.

The nun told Loretta to hand out the holy books with pictures of Baby Jesus and the penitent faces of children kneeling in the confession box. There were very few of these books, so we only got one on each desk. Loretta kept her arm around the book on our desk, the same way I did when I didn't want her to look at my sums. The Home Babies got no books at all. The lesson was about confession. We had to answer questions about venial and mortal sins so we would know what sins to confess.

"Mary Blake, tell me a venial sin you are going to tell the priest when you make your first confession."

"I took sugar from the sugar bowl when Mammy wasn't watching."

The nun's eyes crinkled up. "You stole sugar."

"I didn't, I only took it."

"Make sure to tell the priest you are impertinent and bold in class."

I was going to answer back, "I don't know what impertinent means." but remembered I wanted to go to the yard to ask Brigid about Liam.

"Loretta, what venial sins will Úna McNulty have to tell the priest?"

Loretta looked at Noeleen Pitt and Noeleen whispered to her so loud that everyone heard except Sr Ignatius.

"She copies her sums down wrong from the board."

Loretta stood up and shouted out, "She copies her sums down wrong from the board."

I was going to say, "That's not a sin, it's short sight." but I managed to stop myself in time. After getting Loretta to tell all the sins the girls on the bad side would have to confess, the nuns asked her to collect the books.

When the class stood up to make a line, I sat in my desk until Loretta was nearly out the door. I took my hankie from my sleeve and put it to my nose. Pretending I was wiping my nose, I let the lump of bread and jam fall into my other hand and stood up. The children on the bad side had to stay sitting until the last one from the good side was in the line. On the way out, I shoved my closed fist to Brigid and mouthed, "For Liam." and then pretended to trip. I shoved the bread under her desk near her feet.

Outside, I wanted to go over to Home Babies part of the yard to ask about Liam, but Loretta and her gang made a line, like ring-a-ring-a-roses around me and Kait and Úna. We couldn't break out unless we pushed them and then we'd be in trouble, so we sat on our hunches and played shop. I was thinking if Liam was sick, he'd be in bed. I was not big enough to look over the Home's wall, so even if he was lying near a window, I wouldn't be able to see him, so I stopped thinking about him and listened to what Úna was saying.

Barm Breac & The Banshee

"Nan is making a barm breac for us this evening," Úna said.

"Are you coming, Arlene?"

"Course I am. What's barm breac?"

"A currant cake with the ring in it, silly goose."

"It has everything, the ring, the coin and currants."

"Why?"

"That's why," Kait said.

Úna said, "It's for Ducking Night. They are making it to know who is getting married this year."

"Will they give us some today?"

"They might."

"I wish Nanna would let me use the tongs to put the sods on the lid," Kait said.

The nannas didn't have a range. They baked the cakes on the fire, in a black, iron pot on top of the grate. Nan, even though she couldn't see, rattled among the lumps of turf in the fire with a long-handled tongs. She'd pick up the hot sods and place them on the lid so that way the cake was crusty on the top and on the bottom but soft in the middle. The nannas made round cakes of white and brown bread all the time. They cut a cross in the middle so they could break it into quarters with their hands. When it was baked, they left it on the windowsill to cool. They only use the knife to cut it into slices and to butter it.

As soon as class was finished, we raced across the road and down past the bank on the corner playing 'Tick'. Úna was 'It' and she was trying to catch me or Kait, but we were too fast for her. We sped past St Jarlath's Avenue and when we were halfway up Clonthu Hill, Kait stopped and said, "Can ye smell the cake?" That gave Úna a chance to tip her on the back and Kait was 'It'. She came after me, so I galloped faster and burst into Nanny Ward's house.

Nan Gormley and Nanny were standing in front of the fire with their skirts lifted at the back, because the nannas always stood like that to warm their backsides. Nanny was saying, "Mary, as true as God is in heaven, I saw the Banshee last night…" as I skidded to a halt, but Nanny was like Loretta and tell-taled to Nan and Prince that I nearly knocked her into the fire.

"Would you whist, *a cailín dana*. Are ya trying to push me into the fire and kill me, you villain."

Nanny Ward started laughing and said, "*Tráth*, when I saw the Fairy Woman last night, I never thought for a minute it was yourself she was coming for, Mary."

Nan laughed and answered, "She'll be waiting a long time before I'll go with her Molly, but I'm telling you, she has great *meas* on you."

"What makes you say that, Mary?"

"Yourself is the only one who sees her, the rest of us have to do with hearing her."

"Nanny, what do people see the banshee for?" I asked.

"Ah, a girleen, she comes to tell us she is taking one of ours to the Otherworld with her.

"Well, I didn't see or ever hear her."

"The banshee only comes to the family where one of them is going die, *a grá*," Nan said.

"Do you mean if Mammy or Daddy or me was going to die, the banshee would come to our house, Nan?"

"That's right."

"She hasn't time to be going around to the whole town, so she only goes to the family where someone is going to die."

I was thinking there is only three in my family and I didn't want her to take any of us.

Nanny Ward saw the worry on my face and said, "Arlene, there's no heed for you to be worrying about the banshee, she only comes for auld ones like meself and Nan, even though, I'd be thinking she wouldn't be interested in you, Mary, seeing as you're as blind as a bat."

"Arrah, I might be blind but I'm not deaf, Molly. I can hear as good as the next. The banshee was lamenting last night."

"It was only the *seordán*, you *óinseach*," Nanny answered back, hearing well what Nan had said. Sometimes we had to shout at Nanny but other times she heard us, even when we didn't want her to. Nan was always blind. It didn't bother her because she could hear the kettle singing on the fire. She lifted it off the hook with a cloth and pour it in on top of the tea leaves in a big teapot she left on the hob. Nanny Ward told us Nan was a great tea-leaf reader before she lost the sight. Now she only knitted socks and shooed the hens out with the twig. Nanny helped turn the heel when she got to the heel part because you needed to put some stiches on another needle and knit with three needles until the heel was turned. She gave the socks to Mick the Sticks because none of her socks were the same length. Some were very long and some very short and Mick didn't mind if the two socks weren't the same length, like his legs weren't.

Nan's dog was Prince. His job was to bark and pull at the bottom of Nan's long black skirt when there was something in the way, so Nan wouldn't fall. She put her hand on his neck and got him to lead her slowly back to her house, which was stuck onto Nanny Ward's one. We followed behind, knowing she would give us a dropeen of tay and a slice of bread. Biting through the butter with the sweet, condensed milk and soft bread, licking the sticky, sweet drops dripping down the sides was like having dessert after dinner on Sunday. We passed Nan's wide, tin mug with a big handle at the side, where your whole hand could fit in, around among us, drinking sups of tea out of it.

Nan put on the radio because she had the free one blind people get. It was plugged into the place where the bulb should be. Prince knew he had to be careful and not go near the black cord hanging down or let Nan near it. Afterwards we ran out and stared screaming because Prince was chasing us and putting his paws up on our shoulders as though he was 'It'.

Before it got really dark, we went home. I lived nearer to Clonthu Hill than Úna and Kait. They went to the station and took the shortcut up the tracks while I galloped through Kilmartin Road to Sligo Road and then crossed over to Suileen Lane.

I burst in the door. Mammy said my tea was waiting for me in the kitchen. My tummy was full of the soda bread and I wasn't able to eat anything. Mammy kept looking at me and when Daddy came home, she said, "The child isn't well, William."

"What wrong with the wee lass?"

"She's all flushed and not eating."

"When the wee one doesn't eat, that surely is a bad sign," he covered my forehead down to my nose with his hand. "No fever, Dervla. She's as right as rain."

He bent to pick me up, but Mammy ruined our fun by saying, "Don't get her all worked up before she goes to bed, William. She's bad enough without you making her worse."

"No horseplay then, only Pudsy Ryan before she goes to bed."

Mammy nodded her head but didn't smile. She went to the back kitchen. She came back with a small saucepan in her hand. "Mary, I'll make some coca for you to drink before you go to bed."

While Mammy was boiling the milk, Daddy got the magazine called The Far East. It was full of writing and pictures of black babies, priests, nuns and people from places that were different to Drumbron. The pages at the end were for children.

"Arlene, let's read Pudsy Ryan while Mammy is rattling in the kitchen," Daddy sat me on his lap, and we laughed at Pudsy who was a silly goose. Before Daddy piggy-backed me up the stairs to bed and helped me say my prayers, Mammy washed me in the tin basin.

During the night, screeching like the wind that cries through the trees when there is a storm, woke me up. Shaking I sank down in the bed. I wanted to put my hands over my ears to shut out the piercing sound but was afraid to move from under the blankets. The wailing was getting nearer and nearer, making the hairs on my arms go prickly. Long drawn-out sobs wrapped in whispers and screeches – the same as music from the bagpipes but loud and squeaky like the time I stood on the cat's tail – were outside the window. I heard tapping on the pane of glass. I clenched my eyes shut and pressed my back into the tick, trying to sink in a space among the feathers, frightened, knowing the banshee was outside.

I didn't want to see the fairy woman's white face with her wild hair blowing all over the place and her bony fingers holding the comb, looking in at me. She might be here to take me or Mammy or Daddy back to the Otherworld. I screamed, "Go away, banshee, I won't let you take Mammy or Daddy." My voice was wobbly. I knew the banshee would only laugh, so I closed my mouth tight, swallowed all the spit in it, put my chin down on my neck like when I put a puss on me, and pressed my elbows into the tick and make my back move up. My voice sounded different and I shouted, "Clear off to a different house, you *óinseach*. Go to a house with plenty of brothers and sisters and nannas and granddaddies. At school there are girls with first cousins and cousins once removed. Leave my daddy and mammy alone, you bold banshee." Mammy was standing beside my bed and I asked her, "Mammy, do you hear the banshee?"

"Whist." Mammy sat on the bed and said, "Whist." again. She touched my forehead with her hand and muttered, "Fever. Mary you are having a nightmare, a bad dream."

"Mammy, listen to the crying. It's the banshee."

"No, Mary. It's only a fox crying."

Mammy took me to their room and put me in the bed. Daddy was in the barracks so I wrapped my arms around Mammy's neck and fell asleep, but inside me, I knew it was the banshee and told the fairy woman I would pull her hair if she tried to take any of my family. Nanny Ward and Nan Gormley had said the banshee cries out to tell you someone in your family is going to die.

I woke up lovely and cosy between Mammy and Daddy. I had stopped the banshee from taking any of us. Daddy got up before us to light the fire, so the kitchen would be warm when Mammy got up. When I went downstairs,

I didn't want to eat my porridge and said, "I'm not going to school."

"What nonsense is that?" Mammy said looking vexed.

"I have to mind ye from the banshee." I was stamping my feet and putting on the biggest puss I knew how to make but Daddy pretended he didn't notice. His bike had a flat tyre and he wheeled it out to the garden to blow it up with the pump, while Mammy said, "Mary, *a stoirín beag*, you'll have to stop your *rámhaille*. There is no such thing as the banshee. It's auld women's talk and not a word of truth in it."

"I'm not going to school, do you hear me? Well, Mammy, heed me."

"Mary, how dare you speak like that. The next time you do, I'll wring your neck."

I had to be careful, so I bit my bottom lip hard so no bold words could come out of my mouth and only said, "Tell Daddy to pump his bike in here, in case the banshee takes him."

"That's enough out of you, a girl. There was me thinking that when I left Connemara and the old ways, I'd hear no more nonsense about the Otherworld."

"Daddy, Daddy." I jumped up and ran towards the front door, but Mammy held me. "Mammy, the Banshee came last night to tell us one of the family is going to die. Kiss my heart and swear to die, I heard her last night."

"Can't you see we are all here, no one died."

"Mammy, I thought the banshee came to let you know someone is going to die and the Ghost of Bower comes for the spirit of the person when they are dead?"

"The right name is the Coster not the Ghost of Bower."

"How do you know, Mammy?"

"I heard my mother say it."

"Did my nanna know about the banshee?"

"Some said she had the Second Sight and was in touch with The Others, but it was only *piseogs*."

"What's the Second Sight, Mammy?"

"Seeing things other people don't. When you were a baby people used to say it wasn't your first time around."

"Why did they say that?"

"You were a very knowing baby, and as my mother had the Second Sight, people thought her gift had been passed on to you but as I said, it's only *piseogs*."

"I'm not a baby now, Mammy."

"No, you're nearly six. Your birthday is just around the corner."

"When will I be six?"

"Around Ducking night. My mother said babies born around Oíche Samhain ate a bit of the Salmon of Knowledge and that makes them very knowing."

"Well, I know more than the other children who are all nearly six." I was thinking of Loretta who still didn't know the two and the other two with a cross at the side was four.

"Sometimes I think you'd be better off in not knowing so much."

For all the pusses I put on, in the end, Daddy brought me to school, but Liam wasn't with Brigid.

The nun warned us the priest would be coming in soon to ask us questions for our First Holy Communion and Confession. She didn't want us to make a show of her and was going to test us before we went out for playtime.

"Mary Blake, what is the difference between venial sin and mortal sin?"

"Mortal sins are big, big sins and venial sins are only small ones."

"Is stealing sugar a mortal sin?"

"A pinch of sugar is small, Sister, so it's a venial one."

She shook her head and looked cross. Loretta put up her hand. "Yes dear?"

"May I go to the toilet, please?"

"Of course, my dear. Noeleen Pitt you go with Loretta.

Sister Ignatius kept asking the same questions over and over again. After Loretta and Noeleen came back, we made the line to go to the yard. I looked at Brigid, but she kept her eyes down and was biting her lower lip like Liam had done.

In the line on the way out, I pretended to trip. Brigid raised her eyes and I mouthed, "Where's Liam?"

She whispered back, "Liam is in the infirmary."

I didn't know what the infirmary meant and wanted to ask her in the yard, but she was in a different part, away from us. I played with Úna and Kait and thought when Daddy comes, I'll ask him what infirmary means.

Daddy was outside on Cork Road with Mr Delaney and Mr Fitzgerald. They were saying Galway had a good chance of winning the championship. I knew children are to be seen but not heard, so I kept quiet and watched Mick the Sticks. He was lifting himself along the path on his crutches. He used the crutches to swing his body a bit forward and land on his one leg. The gone leg had the empty trousers tied at the knee with a safety pin. The knuckles of his hands were white and up a bit from the rest of his fists because he was pressing down really hard and tight on the little sticks that went across the middle of the two sides, like the middle bar in the goal post in the pitch. The long, side sticks went down to the ground and joined together into one at the bottom. It changed into a thick, round, black peg, like the leg of a chair. The top part of the crutches, covered with a thin pillow of brown leather, were under his oxters and were pushing his shoulders up near to his neck.

I smiled at him, but like the Home Babies, he kept his eyes down. When I turned back to Daddy, I heard Mr Delaney saying, "...the priest was there early this morning."

Mr Fitzgerald said, "Anointed and ready to meet her maker. Tragic but now it's our duty to make sure the children are safe, so Will..."

Daddy felt me pressing against his leg and caught my hand and started to move away but he looked at Mr Fitzgerald and Mr Delaney and said, "Rest assured, what has to be done will be done."

"What children, Daddy?" I wanted to know but Daddy didn't answer. Instead he said he would bet me a sweet that Mammy had bought a pink dress in Sligo.

"Did you go with her, Daddy?"

"Mammy went with Mr Delaney because I was in the barracks."

"You were talking to Mr Delaney and he told you."

He laughed and ruffled my hair.

"And that is why you know."

When we got home, Mammy was sitting in the parlour, looking smashing in a new pink twinset. She was holding a silver tube and twisting it. A lipstick came up. She put it to her lips and painted them red like jelly.

"Mammy, Mammy, did you buy me anything?" I screamed running towards her.

"Manners, Mary," she said, taking a small, white paper bag of tiny, square sweets from her handbag.

I stopped running because I knew she wouldn't give me the lovely sweets from Woolworth's if I didn't have manners but I couldn't help saying to Daddy, "Look, Mammy went for a spin to Sligo in Mr Delaney's car and got me a bag of sweets."

"Is there one for me, Arlene?"

"Of course there is, Daddy, and one for Mammy and for Mr Delaney," I said, and Mammy smiled and gave me the bag. I took one out and gave it to Daddy. I was doing the same for Mammy, but she said a nice girl offers the bag and lets the other pick the sweet themselves, so I did that. Daddy was looking at Mammy, so I said, "Mammy got new lipstick, Daddy!" and put a sweet in my pocket for Liam while he was saying, "Dervla, what do you think if I get the squad car and we go to Trafada when the weather gets warm?"

"That's a grand idea. The sea air would do Mary the world of good."

Daddy was standing behind Mammy and put his hands on her shoulders. She shrugged them off and said, "I still have a headache from the night Mary gave me."

"She was restless last night but she's fine now, aren't you lassie?"

"I am, Daddy."

Mammy didn't think I was fine because she said, "I'll sleep in with her tonight, William, so I don't have to be getting up all the time."

"Ach, there's no need for that. Arlene, come on, let's have a game of ball to tire you out for the night."

"Rough Stuff, Daddy?" I asked. Rough stuff was great to play because you just had to kick the ball around on the ground with your feet and not worry about kicking it in the air.

From the garden, I saw Úna pushing the pram along Suileen Lane with her small brother Brendan and her baby sister Teresa. I waved to her. Our housekeeper, Mrs McLoughlin, tapped on the window to call us in for tea. She was talking about Nora McHugh, who had left the world while her baby was coming into it and blessing herself said, "God between and all harm but it's an awful thing to happen." Mammy nodded her head and said nothing but looked at Daddy.

After tea, as soon as Mrs McLoughlin had cleaned up and went home to Maura and Catherine, Daddy changed into his uniform. I wanted to go with him to the barracks, but he said he had to go to the priest's house on business. Mammy was hanging up her new clothes in the wardrobe, so I pulled her skirt and said I wanted to go with Daddy. With a vexed look she told me to go and play, so I traipsed down the stairs, dragging my feet and went out to the garden with a puss on me, but then I saw Úna coming back from her long walk along Suileen Lane and I ran out to her. She let me push the pram.

That night, when I went to bed, I remembered the sweet in my pocket for Liam and thought I had the best Mammy and Daddy in the whole, wide world for giving me sweets.

The next morning when I came into the kitchen, I saw Mammy looking at Daddy with her eyes opened wide. "He took the pitchfork to you. What's the world coming to when the priests and the Gardaí are treated like that."

"Dervla, look who's up early and bright?" Daddy said in the voice that meant they were talking about something I wasn't meant to hear.

"You're looking better, will I boil an egg for you?"

"No, Mammy, I'll only have porridge." I ate all my porridge and a slice of toast and went off to school with Daddy on the bike.

The Infirmary

I looked towards the bad side when the Home Babies were dragging themselves in. Liam wasn't among them. I wanted to catch Brigid's eye to ask her if her brother was still sick, but her eyes were looking at the floor the whole time.

After looking at the cat on the mat and talking about the children kneeling in front of the confession box, we made a line and went out to play. In the yard, Brigid wouldn't look at me. I was going over to where she was with the sweet for Liam. Loretta saw me and said she would tell the nun, so I stayed with Úna and Kait. Back in the classroom, I kept turning around to look at Brigid.

"Mary Blake, have you worms?" Sr Ignatius said in a loud voice and all heads turned to look at me.

"I don't," I said in a bold voice.

"The way you are moving in your seat makes me think you have."

I didn't answer.

"Is all the sugar you steal from the sugar bowl for the worms?"

"It isn't and I don't have worms," I muttered low and the nun didn't hear me.

"Sit quiet and stop moving in your seat, Giddy Goat."

Regina Burke started saying "Giddy Goat." under her breathe and Loretta was skitting, making her head bob up and down and making her curly hair wobble. I reached out my fingers and pulled one of them out, because Úna's cousin, Lina Gormley, told us Loretta really had straight hair.

Lina Gormley, Úna's first cousin, was like Mrs McLoughlin who worked for us, only Lina worked for the Fitzgerald's and was called a service-girl. She polished the shoes every evening and set the table for breakfast before she went home. That was because the following morning she had to be in the house very early to make the breakfast for the family. She said the Fitzgerald's only eat shop-bought white sliced pan and she had to cut off the crusts for Loretta as well as doing her curls. She told us every night she wet Loretta's hair and wrapped newspaper around the wet bits. She did this in the bathroom because the Fitzgerald's had a bathroom and didn't have to wash in the kitchen, like everyone else in Drumbron.

When Loretta got up in the morning, Lina took off all the papers, so Loretta's head was full of cork-screw ringlets. Mrs Fitzgerald wanted Loretta to look like Shirley Temple. I was going to show everyone the curls were not real, and she had straight hair, so catching the end of one of Loretta's curls, I pulled it softly towards me and then let it bounce back, thinking if I kept pulling the same curly it might stop being a curl and fall down like Kait's hair. Loretta didn't know what I was doing, and she screamed, "Stop it."

"Mary Blake, I am at the end of my tether with you," said the nun, getting up but I moved quicker and was over on the bad side before she reached me.

I rushed to the back row and sat in Liam's place. I waited until Sister Ignatius' mouth stopped hissing and saying pulling another girl's hair was a new sin I had to confess, before I edged towards Brigid and whispered, "Where's Liam?" Her chest heaved. I was afraid she would start bawling. I looked down and pointed my finger at the floor. I then bent my head towards my shoes. She did the same. We looked into each other eyes. They were a light blue, different from mine and my mammy's.

Her bottom lip trembled as she mouthed, "Liam is sick. He…he… won't wake up." I wished I had some bread and jam but I opened my hand so she could see the small sweet in it. She didn't take it, so I left it on the floor.

"Mary Blake, what are you doing with your head under the desk?"

"Nothing sister, my hankie fell."

"Pick it up and sit still."

I crossed my fingers and wished Liam went to the dispensary to see the doctor. I could talk to him there, so after school I was going to ask Úna to show me where the dispensary was in case Liam was there.

The class dragged on. I kept looking at Brigid wanting her to look at me. From the side of her face, I saw she had a dimple in her chin too. Before the only people I knew with dimples were Daddy and me. The one time she looked at me, there was water in her eyes ready to fall, like the drops of holy water that falls from the fat stick when the priest sprinkles the coffin in the middle aisle at the funerals. Her face was white like the loose, lacy blouse altar boys wear over the black dress for serving Mass. The *grá* came on me and I wanted to hug her, and I wanted her to hug me, like Mammy had hugged me last night. The ruler tapping on my desk made me look up. Sister Ignatius was standing right beside me.

"Mary Blake, when I ask a child a question, I expect an answer."

"Yes, Sister."

"Yes, Sister what?"

"To the question you asked me, Sister," she turned towards the good side.

"Loretta stand up and make the line."

I started to get up.

"Mary Blake, where do you think you are going? Get back into your seat this minute. How dare you think you can go and play after the way you pulled Loretta's hair."

Loretta stuck her tongue out at me and seemed delighted I was being chastised. I didn't care because after school me, Kait and Úna were going up Clonthu Hill. We might even be cutting out the eyes and nose and mouth in the turnips Nan and Nanny were going to buy for us so we could make lanterns for Ducking Night. It would soon be Ducking Night and I was going to slope down the stairs to go out with my pals that night because Úna said it was great fun going out in the dark with the candle stuck in the turnips with the faces.

After the yard, the line came back in. Brigid didn't look at me, but Loretta did. I couldn't stick my tongue out at her because the nun was beside her. When class was over, I went out our door to the cloakroom, where our coats were hanging. I waited for Úna and Kait there.

"Úna, where's the dispensary?"

"It's stuck in a corner near the post office. Why do you want to know?"

"That's why. Is it open now?"

"No, it's only open in the mornings."

"Who goes there?"

"Everyone. It's full always and only the old women can sit on the bench."

"What bench?"

"The one against the wall. Daddy said we should let the old people sit on the bench because they get tired standing against the wall."

"Do you stand against the wall?"

"Sometimes but other times Daddy holds me in his arms when I am very sick."

It was no good going to the dispensary. It was closed, so I'd just go up Clonthu Hill to cut the faces in the turnips. We had a race to see who would get to the Woods Hospital first. I won. I put my hand on the gate a second before Kait did. I wondered where Úna was and turned around to see her trailing behind, with her hands pressed close to her ears to keep her glasses from falling off. Kait was galloping down the road shouting, "Whoever put their hand on the railway gate in the next winner." I nearly caught up to her, but she won.

We waited for Úna. She was not running fast. I suppose she was afraid she'd bang into something. After the station, we walked and talked until we got to Nanny Ward's house. Nan Gormley and Prince were already sitting by the fire.

"*Tráth*, ye're just the girls I wanted to see. Will ye bring me in a brosan of turf, *a grá*." The three of us galloped out to the back door to the reek of turf.

"Arlene and you, Kait, stick out yer arms."

"Úna, wait a sec. I have to take my cardigan off, so Mammy doesn't see the biteens of turf on the sleeves." Once Mammy found the hay bits that are on the sides of some sods and asked me how I got wisps of dried grass on my jumper. I told her it must have been when I was with Daddy in the football pitch.

Úna stacked the sods on our outstretched arms. When the heap reached our chins, we plodded back into the kitchen and lowered ourselves onto our hunkers near the fireplace. Úna then took the turf off our arms and piled it beside the open hearth. There were black hobs at the side of the grate. We always wanted to sit on them, but Nan and Nanny wouldn't let us, saying we might fall into the fire, so we ended up fighting to sit on the three-legged stool. It was great being in front of the ashy sods and looking at the big kettle hanging from a chain with a hook at the end. The nannas filled the kettle with water from the pump that was near Nuns field and boiled it on the fire.

"Do ya want a sup of tay, *a stoirín beag*?" they asked before handing us a wide tin mug they used to drink tea out of. I took one of the white, clay pipes with bacca in it.

"Nanny, I want to smoke your pipe."

"*A grá*, ya have time enough for that when you grow up."

While we were drinking the tea, Nan said, "Mary, the heart was crossways within me last night with the way the banshee was looking in at me through the pane of glass." She pointed to the window.

"Molly, the banshee must have great *grá* for you because you're the only one she lets see her, but you're right in that she was around, sure me head was light with the wailing of her."

"That's two with Auld Packy Duggan and Nora McHugh. Wonder who the third will be?"

When the banshee came and cried, the whole town would be wondering who the three people were who were going to die. The nannas said death came in threes and started talking about the woman who had died that morning.

"Poor Nora McHugh. It won't be long before the Coster Bower is rattling past their door."

"Cathal is demented. Sure, it's hard for a man to lose his wife but we know it's more than the wife that will be taken from him."

"We do."

"The priest was there giving poor Nora the Last Rites."

"If Kelly had got there as quick, she might be still among us."

"Indeedin you're right, and there'd be no need for the Coster Bower to be harnessing his horses."

"What's the Coster Bower, Nanny?"

"Something you're better off not seeing, a girl."

"Why?"

"It would put the fear of God into you."

"Why?"

"It's driven by a headless driver."

"If he has no head, how does he see?"

"He has a head but not on his shoulders."

"Where does he have his head?"

"Held in his hand."

"That's stupid. Why doesn't he put it on his neck like everyone?"

"Because he needs it as a lantern to guide the horses in the dark."

"Is there a candle stuck in his head like our turnips?"

"There isn't. The eyes are as bright as fire of hell and light the way."

"Like your fire?"

"Brighter."

"How many horses does the coach have?"

"Six."

"Does he whip the horses like Mick the Sweep."

"He doesn't, the six black horses pulling the coach know the house Dullahan wants to go to."

"Is the headless driver's name Dullahan?"

"It's what people call him."

"Úna, *a rua*, take this *cailín dubh* out to play. She's making me head light with all the questions she asks."

Instead of playing, we went home because Úna had to mind her baby brother and sister.

I slept through the night without waking Mammy. The next morning, she was looking happy eating breakfast. Daddy was the one who had a funny face on him. Mammy told him he was only doing his duty. He gave her that look that meant he didn't want me to know what they were talking about.

At school, we did the same thing every day. We saw the cat on the mat, we did our sums on the slates and we learned what venial sins were. On Thursday it was different for me. I went to elocution lessons with Miss Clark. She knocked on our door and opened it and waited there until Sr Ignatius called out names from a list in her hand. Me and another few girls from the good side stood up and made a line and left with the elocution teacher. Loretta and her pals didn't go because Miss Clark went to their houses to teach them how to speak. We waited outside the door of each classroom while Miss Clark got the other pupils.

In the big hall there was a stage with wooden steps in front of it. We made a choir by standing on the steps in rows one behind the other. The teacher taught us how to speak properly and we learned a poem about a girl called Matilda. Úna and Kait said I was lucky, and they would love to go to elocution with me, but their mammies didn't have the money for it. I told them the dump was better and I was dying to go there.

After class, only me and Kait went because Úna had to go home to mind the small ones. In the dump, I found green glass and a broken plate. I smashed it with a stone to break it into small pieces.

"Them smithereens will buy you plenty of things when we play shop," Kate said. I carried them in my dress, like Nan carried the waste in her apron for the hens.

As we were coming back, we saw Úna pushing the big-bellied pram with her baby brother and sister. We called her and showed her all the money I found.

"Arlene, you have to find a place where you can hide it."
"Why?"
"In case anyone steals it."
"Where can I hide it?"
"Near your house, then you can get it quick when you need it."

We walked back to Suileen Lane, past my house and found a great hiding place under a stone.

"Now you can wheel the pram, cos your hands are free."

The three of us took turns pushing the babies, Brendan and Teresa. At Railway Terrace I went back home for my tea. When I got in the door Mammy looked at my dress and said she didn't know how I could get so dirty. Daddy didn't come home for tea. When I was ready for bed, he wasn't there to piggy-back me up the stairs.

"Where's Daddy?"

"That Cathal McHugh is drunk out of his head and throwing abuse at the bishop and the Gardaí so Daddy has to stay in the barracks.

"Will he be home tomorrow?"

"He will. As soon as they get that awful man sent to Ballinacora, he'll be home."

Sickness

Brigid didn't come to school so I couldn't ask her about Liam. I was very tired and wanted to go home. I told Úna and Kait I was tired and didn't want to go to the nannas to get the lanterns ready for Ducking Night.

"Don't worry, Arlene. We'll cut out the insides of your turnip."

"Alright, but don't do the eyes or nose or mouth."

"No, you can do them yourself the next day."

When I got home, Mammy said I didn't look well. I didn't feel hungry and wanted to go to bed. She felt my forehead and then got me ready. We went upstairs. In bed, my eyes kept closing when we were saying our prayers and I dozed off without blessing myself at the end of the prayers.

During the night, I woke up at the sound of the cart's wheels and a horse neighing. Mammy was asleep in her room, so I got up and went to her in her bed to ask her if Mick the Sweep was coming to clean our chimney.

"Mammy, do you hear the rattling of the wheels?"

"Mary, stop your nonsense about the Coster Bower."

When Mammy said that, I knew straight away who was outside our house. I jumped up onto the bed to be closer beside her and mind her better. I wouldn't let the Coster

Bower take my Mammy. The horse and carriage didn't stop, it kept going. Mammy was safe but Daddy?

"Mammy where is Daddy?"

"He's playing cards with Dr Kelly, so stop your *rámhaille*."

But I couldn't stop thinking about what the nannas said about how Nora McHugh was dead and Packy Duggan was on his way out. That meant there was still another person to die because death comes in threes. I tried to ask Mammy if she knew who else was dying but she said, "Whist!" every time I started to speak. I fell asleep with 'whist' in my ears.

The next morning, Mammy was cross with me. "Mary, I have had enough of your *rámhaille* about the Coster Bower. I want to hear no more out of you about banshees and the like."

I insisted I had heard the wheels and the neighing of the horse and burst out before she could hush me. "Mammy, I heard the carriage last night. They were coming to get one of us."

"They weren't. We are all alive and well."

"But Daddy?"

"He's in the barracks. And you and I are here in bed looking at each other, all the family is fine."

"Mammy, does the banshee come to let you know someone is going to die and the Coster Bower comes for the spirit of the person when they are dead?"

"Mary, what did I just say?"

"But…"

"I don't want another word out of you about ghosts."

Mammy got up but told me to stay in bed because I was very hot.

"I want to go to the market with you, Mammy."

"Mary, you're not well. I'll get Dr Kelly to come and have a look at you."

"I want to go downtown with you."

"I was going to take you with me to the funeral of Nora McHugh, but you're better off in bed until Dr Kelly sees you."

"Mammy, the last funeral we went to was Mr McLoughlin's."

"That's right but poor Nora McHugh left a small family behind. Daddy has a hard day ahead of him."

"Will there be a fight? Are the McHugh's tinkers?"

"No, they aren't, but there are decisions to be made about the children."

"What decisions about them?"

"Nothing. It's not something a child needs to know. I'll bring you up a cup of tea and toast."

I stayed in bed. When I lay down, my throat tickled, and I started coughing. At teatime Dr Kelly came. He examined my chest with a thing hanging from his ears and looked in my ears. He told Mammy to keep me in bed because he thought I was getting the measles.

"Dervla, the dispensary is crowded, children coming in coughing, with sore eyes and high temperatures. The best place for this little one is in bed. Give her plenty to drink and keep the curtains drawn."

From then on, every morning Dr Kelly popped in to see how I was. Mammy told him I wouldn't have the chicken soup she made, I pushed Daddy away when he wanted to read me stories, and he couldn't even coax me to eat the chocolate he brought home. It was dark with white cream in the middle. I just wanted to sleep.

Then one day I wasn't tired and wanted to get up. Mammy and Daddy were smiling but Dr Kelly said, "She's not out of the woods yet." He was right because that night I was boiling hot and sweating. My hair was stuck to my head, it soaked the pillow and the sheets. My nightdress was drenched with sweat and the sheets were as well. Mammy changed them. She stayed bent over the bed and kept putting cool, wet face towels on my forehead until they became warm. Then she took them off and replaced them with another cold one. My nightdress was wet again. She changed it and the sheets and pillowcase. Daddy was in the barracks, so Mrs McLoughlin was helping Mammy. I was sort of asleep, knowing what was happening but not wanting to move when Mammy needed to change the sheets.

Daddy came home. He sat down for a few minutes, then he got up again, biting the back of his fist. The next time the sheets got wet and Mammy needed to change them, she got him to lift me out of the bed. During the night she had to change the sheets and my nightdress again. Daddy went for Dr Kelly.

"It is what I feared, Will, a bad dose of measles."

"Measles, Brian? But where are the spots."

"They'll appear. You know, Dervla, you'd make a great nurse the way you are handling this."

"I'm only trying to keep her cool, the fever is burning her up."

"You're doing the only thing that can be done by wiping her down with the cool, damp cloth." He told them once the fever broke, the spots would appear.

After sleeping and waking, tossing and turning for a long time, I stopped boiling. Mammy examined my face and smiled. She told Daddy to get his shaving mirror. When I looked into it, my face was covered in spots like the side of a trout. Mammy and Daddy were kissing and hugging me. I sat up in bed and had some tea and toast. They were smiling and laughing and looking at each other as though they wanted to cry.

"Arlene how old are you?"

"Five, Daddy."

"Mammy, tell this wee lass how old she is."

"She's not a little girl anymore but a big one. Mary, it was your birthday two weeks ago when you were sick. Now you are six."

And big like Úna and Kait.

Daddy handed Mammy a box and a parcel wrapped in striped paper.

"Do you want to open your first present?" Mammy said as she helped me sit up in bed and put the box in front of me.

I lifted the lid and couldn't stop the scream coming out of me and my hands were shaking, afraid to touch the pair of patent shoes with a strap across the front and a buckle at the side to tie them. I looked at Mammy and Daddy to make sure they were for me. Mammy nodded her head as she took out one of the beautiful shoes and gave it to me. Touching the smooth, shiny black with the tip of my finger, I asked, "Mammy, can I wear them tomorrow to school. I want everyone to see them."

"Mary, you'll wear them when we go to Mass."

"But Mammy, Loretta wears hers to school every day only not when it's raining. I want to wear mine too."

"You will, but they would get ruined in this weather. We'll wait until spring."

"Can I not wear them tomorrow?"

"Dr Kelly wants you to stay at home for another good while."

"I want to go to school," I said as I started to tear off the paper around the other present Daddy had given me.

Mammy put her hand on my hands. "Mary, if you rip it off, we can't use the paper again. Let me show you how to open it without tearing it to bits."

I was dying to see the present and didn't give a sugar about the fancy paper but I had to wait. Mammy held the beginning of the Sellotape with her finger and thumb and peeled it off carefully. I bit my bottom lip and crossed my fingers for her to hurry up because instead of pushing it back quickly, she took ages, folding it like a sheet before I was able to see. First, I saw a picture. Then I saw it was the cover of a book with children running in a park.

Underneath that book there was a fat book with a hard cover, like the holy ones Sister Ignatius told Loretta to give out at catechism class. Two books, a fat and a thin one was Daddy's present.

"Arlene, this book is for colouring," Daddy said picking up the light book with the children in the park.

"Daddy, I have no crayons or paints."

"Pet, I'll be standing at Byrne's tomorrow morning waiting for it to open. It won't be long until we are colouring in the pictures."

"William, wait until she is feeling better."

"But I'm better Mammy. Daddy, what's the other book, I want to see before I get up to try on my new shoes."

"It's a fairy tale book, so we can read about the elves and pixies."

"Let me see, Daddy!" I squealed with excitement.

The fairies in the book were not real fairies. They didn't live in fairy rings in Nuns Field or take people's souls. They were called elves. They had magic wands, pointy ears and wore dresses like a communion veil.

"Daddy, will you go to Byrne's soon? I want to colour all the pages."

"You'll have to wait until tomorrow morning, missy."

"Alright, Daddy. I'll try on my new shoes now, if ye don't mind."

They helped me out the bed. My legs were wobbly. The shoes felt heavy and kept my feet weighted to the floor when I tried to walk, but they were smashing, nicer than

Loretta's. I didn't mind when Daddy picked me up and put me back into the bed. Mammy went downstairs and brought up some hot coals in a bucket. With a long tongs she took them out of the bucket and placed them on grate in the small fireplace with the shiny, black fence in front. The room became cosy and I fell asleep.

The next day Mammy made porridge and I ate two spoons of it. Daddy was home at dinner time. When he came into the room, he was holding something behind his back.

"Guess what I have for this little missy?"

"Is it the box of paints, Daddy?"

"You're a clever wee lass."

"Will you stay with me and we'll paint the house on the first page?"

"Alright but we'll need the tray Mammy puts your food on and two jam jars."

"Why two jars, Daddy?"

"You dip your brush into one and wet the paints with it and the other ones is for cleaning the brushes."

It was smashing sitting up in bed and Daddy showing me how to drip the paintbrush into the jar of water and then into a square on the box.

"Daddy, I'm going to paint the sky around the house blue."

"Ach, that will take a while, it's a big sky," Daddy said at the door. He was going downstairs to get a cup of tea. He was right. The square of blue paint was getting small. My brush was making it disappear in the middle. I had finished painting the whole picture of the house and sky when Daddy came back up.

"Daddy, nearly all the blue in the square is gone. When I want to colour another sky, I won't have enough paint to do it." He laughed and said he was going to teach me a trick.

"Arlene, do you see this blue here?" he said pointing to a dark blue like my eyes and Mammy's as well. "If you mix in a bit of white it will become lighter."

I looked at his eyes and said, "Is that what happened to your eyes? Did God run out of Mammy's and my blue colour?"

"What do mean, missy?"

"Your eyes are like this blue with the white. I think God mixed a small biteen of white to make enough paint for your eyes and that's why your eyes are different from Mammy and mine."

"You're as cute as fox, no one else would think of a thing like that," he said laughing, as he called Mammy to tell her what I had said. Mammy said I knew too much for my own good.

When Daddy went back to work, I finished the first page and turned to the next one with the little boy fishing in the river. He had big eyes and a fringe falling on his forehead. Even though the boy in the picture had nice clothes on, he reminded me of Liam, the boy with the snotty beak from The Home. I painted the book-boy's hair yellow and then mixed the dark blue with a bit of white for his eyes. I coloured the river a dark blue and the fishing brown and the grass green. It looks smashing. I asked Mammy if I could tear out the page and put it on the black mantelpiece over the fireplace where the Sacred Heart picture was hanging.

"I don't know, Mary, if it falls into the grate, we could set the whole place on fire."

"If Daddy put a tack into it, it won't fall."

"Maybe you're right. I'll go down and get one."

I sat up straight in bed to look at the page of the boy. The butter coloured hair and white-blue eyes were like Daddy's, so I called the boy Will. Looking at Will made me wonder if Liam was back at school. Maybe the doctor in the dispensary said he had to stay in bed another good while like Dr Kelly had said about me. I wanted to get up and go to school but Dr Kelly wouldn't hear of it because I wasn't out of the woods yet.

Every morning after Daddy left for the barracks, Mammy brought a basin of water into the room. She washed my face and hands and brushed my hair and made two plaits that hung on each side of my shoulders. After I had my tea and toast, I spent the time colouring my book, waiting for the Angelus to come on the radio downstairs. When the tinkling-booming sounds were over, Mammy would dress me and let me downstairs for dinner because Dr Kelly said I had to take it easy. That meant I could get up during the day but not go outside.

I only minded a small bit because Mrs McLoughlin was rattling about in the kitchen and the radio was on. I heard The Walton's with the man saying, 'Do sing an Irish song'. After dinner and before it got dark, there was a programme for children. The big children wrote to the man and told him plenty of things that he read out. When I could write, I was going to send a letter too.

Christmas

I helped Mammy and Mrs McLoughlin make the Christmas pudding. It was a brown, soft bowl-shaped cake that tasted like Chester cake. The pudding was for dessert on Christmas day. I didn't like the taste of it, but it was great fun helping Mammy and Mrs McLoughlin make it. I grated the breadcrumbs sitting on a clean sheet, spread on the floor, squeezing a bowl between my legs, surrounded by crusts of shop-bought loaves.

I shredded the hard bread into the bowl with a metal grater with tiny, weeny holes that ended in small spikes. The skin on the tips of my fingers could get rubbed off and fall into the bowl if I kept grating when the bread was almost all gone. When I got to near the end of the crust, I put the small biteens to one side, so Mammy could use them for a bread-and-butter pudding. Most of the grated crusts dropped into the bowl but some of the breadcrumbs fell on the sheet. Mammy gathered them up and threw them into the bowl with my crumbs, saying they were clean.

Mammy boiled brown sugar and brandy in a saucepan. When she mixed this water with the raisins, currants and sultanas to the white breadcrumbs, they turned brown. The soggy breadcrumbs were spooned on to a clean dishcloth.

Mammy pulled the four corners of the cloth together in the middle and tied them with thread, changing the guggy mess into a round ball with a floppy ribbon on top. After that, she put the round parcel into a big saucepan with water and left it on the range to simmer all day and all night. Sometimes she moved it to the side of the stove, lifted the lid and poured water from the kettle into the saucepan.

It took us a long time to make the pudding. We started when it was light outside the window and when Mammy put the bowl into the big saucepan on the range, it was dark. We had to put the light on and then it was time for Mrs McLoughlin to go home to Maura and Catherine.

While I was sick at home Mr Delaney came to visit. I didn't like him, but Mammy was delighted and said silly goose things to him.

"John, it's great of you to come to see us. Ah, there was no need for you to buy a cake, sure yourself is enough."

"Dervla, what's a cake compared to the smile and welcome I get?" he said.

"Oh John!" Mammy replied as she poured boiling water from the kettle into the good teapot. She put it on a tray, with slices of caked on a plate, and signalled to Mr Delaney to follow her into the parlour. The weather was getting cold and Mammy always lit a fire in the grate when he came. They liked to go there to talk about big people things. I sat at the kitchen table painting until the light coming in the kitchen window turned grey and was getting ready to go away then I'd call out, "Mammy I can't see."

"Alright, Mary. Come in here."

I left my painting book on the table and went to where they were and heard what they were saying. Mr Delaney brought all the news from around town to Mammy.

Fr Mannion was annoyed because the musical, that was in the Odeon Cinema every Christmastime, had a dance in it with cans and the dancers raises their legs high in the air. In my Irish stepping dance class, we learned to raise our legs a little bit high. But in the French dance, Mr Delaney said the shameless hussies, kicked their legs in the air, screamed and showed their knickers to everyone as they danced back and forth across on the stage with the cans. Mammy was as cross as Mr Delaney. She was nodding her head with a vexed look on her face, when he was saying, "I agree wholeheartedly with the priest that any girl who is brazen enough to raise her leg in the air and show off her knickers –" he stopped and frowned before he continued, "underwear should not be allowed to become a Child of Mary."

"Exactly my feelings, John. Where is the modesty in that?"

"Mammy, when I'm better, can I go to see the girls dancing with the cans on the stage?"

"Mary, how many times have I told you children are seen, not heard? When you are better, you'll go to school and not to see that French can-can dance."

The new Pope was very bold too. He wasn't dancing with cans, but they were always giving out about him.

The two of them kept giving out about people until Mr Delaney stood up and went to the sitting room window. He said, "The night is on us already," and that meant he was leaving.

"Say good night to Mr Delaney. He's off to a sodality meeting."

"Alright. What's a sodality meeting?"

"It's for people who like to pray."

"Where is it?"

"In the parish hall."

"Does Daddy go?"

"He doesn't but he makes sure to go there to play cards."

"He showed me how to play twenty-five."

"That's your father for you. It would be more in his line to teach you to behave like a nice girl."

"He does, he tells me to be a good girl."

"Enough out of you. Will you have a boiled egg for your tea?"

"I want what Daddy is having."

"Corned beef? You want some too?" I didn't know what corned beef was, but I nodded my head. I looked at Mr Delaney, the silly goose, waiting for him to say, "You'll never feel until Christmas is on us and we are plucking the turkey." because that meant he had his overcoat on and was ready to leave.

One evening after Mr Delaney left, I said, "Will Daddy be here soon? I want to show him the page I coloured."

"He will but don't be tormenting him when he gets home. He had enough trouble this morning."

"Was there a tinker's funeral?"

"There wasn't, but that nasty Cathal McHugh was throwing stones at the presbytery's windows."

"Did he break any?"

"He didn't. He was too drunk to take aim."

"Will Daddy put him in jail?"

"That's what Cathal would like, fed and kept here in town with his friends around, but it's in Ballinacora he'll be locked up in."

"Why?"

"To learn a bit of respect for the priests and the bishop."

"How do you know? I didn't see Daddy talking to you since the morning-time?"

"It was Mr Delaney who told me the goings on of that man and the way he can't stand up straight with the amount of drink he takes."

"Mr Delaney knows all the news."

"He takes an interest in what is happening. Whist. I hear Daddy's bike. Sit down and I'll put the eggs on to boil."

Dr Kelly let me back to school on the last day before the Christmas holidays, to see the crib outside Sister Anthony's office. When I was in High Babies with Sister Paul, we made a line and went to look at the big a curly-haired Baby Jesus lying in a box with straw. The statues of Our Lady and St Joseph were kneeling behind the cow and ass because the animals had to be near the baby to blow their breaths on Him and keep Him warm. I wanted to see it again and kept tormenting Mammy to let me go to school and see it. In the end, the doctor said it wouldn't do me any harm if Mr Delaney drove me and Mammy to the school and I wasn't out much in the cold. We went in through the door, looked at the crib and we left straight away. I didn't see my pals Úna, Kait, Brigid or Liam, only the table and the straw.

In the car Mr Delaney said, "Dervla, we'll stop at the Royal Hotel for a Christmas drink." He drove to the hotel on *An Lár* and parked the car in front of the hotel door, so I didn't have to walk in the cold air. I stopped for a second to look at the bulbs of blue, red, green and yellow up in the sky. They were hanging on lines going from one side of the street to the other side near the hotel. I wanted to stay looking at them, wondering would a flying canister shoot across, like in the drapery shop, but Mr Delaney pushed me in through the hotel door.

He walked in front and we followed behind him to a room with a carpet all over the floor, spreading out until it hit the walls. We twisted in and out among round tables and chairs until we were standing in front of a low table near the windows. Mr Delaney pulled it out a bit and we sat in behind it on a long seat with cushions, the same colour as the curtains falling to the ground at the long windows. At the other side of the room, right in front of us there was a woman standing behind a short counter. She lifted a flap and came out and crossed the room to us.

"Howya, John? Great weather for this time of the year."

"Tis indeed. We'll never feel until Christmas is on us and we are plucking the turkey."

"Never said a truer word. In less than a week, we'll all be at Midnight Mass."

"We will indeed."

"The usual for yourself, John, and I suppose a glass of lemonade for this pretty little girl, and Mrs Blake, what will you have?"

"Mrs Blake will be having a glass of sherry and some of your trifle for the young lady, as well as the lemonade."

She went off and after a while a man came carrying a tray and placed a small glass with a leg at the bottom in front of Mammy. It was full of brown coloured water. The lemonade was in a normal glass, but my trifle was in a glass with a leg like Mammy's but bigger. The trifle was like jelly and custard but with wet cake at the bottom and thick cream on top and tiny, coloured beads that Mammy called thousand and ones. Mr Delaney's glass was big and round like Santy's belly, filled with black water and white, sudsy foam on top.

Mammy and Mr Delaney were talking away, so I passed the time looking at the people sitting at the other tables. An old man, who was sitting by the fire, winked at me and then got up and came over to our table. Mr Delaney asked him how he was.

"Better than yourself, John. Sure, I'll see another few Christmases yet."

"You will indeed, Mattie, and pluck many's a turkey."

Mammy had another sherry before we went out to the car. Outside, it was pitch dark with strings of shiny, coloured beads hanging on the neck of street. Someone had switched on the bulbs and they glowed like the fire in the grate. The square was gay and glittery as we drove home.

There were special things to eat at Christmas, like the brown pudding I helped Mammy make. Mrs McLoughlin always made us a Christmas cake so we could celebrate Baby Jesus' birthday on Christmas Day. He was born in a stable. Everyone in Drumbron left the front door open on Christmas Eve, so the Holy Family would have somewhere to spend the night and not have to go back to the stable.

Even though Santa Claus was fat, he didn't come in through the open doors, but he came down the chimney because he was magic and never got stuck in it with his bag of toys. He left me a teddy bear, just like the one I had seen in Byrne's shop, a colouring book, two vests and two knickers and two pairs of socks. When I was upstairs in my bed with Teddy, I looked over at Will on the mantlepiece and wondered what Liam got. Christmas was smashing but I wanted to go back to school and see my pals and tell them about my measles and Teddy. I crossed my fingers so I could go back to school and then I did.

One frosty morning, Maura McLoughlin came to my house to take me to school because she was big. On the way there, she told me she was eleven, her brother Michael was ten, her brother Jim nine, her sister Catherine seven and her brother Paddy was four.

"Maura, do ye have a big, big house like Loretta's, one for ye all to fit in?"

"I suppose we do because there's room for us all and we have a cat too. Mammy and Paddy sleep downstairs in the front room, I'm in the upstairs front room with Catherine and Michael and Jim are in the back room."

"Have you a parlour?"

"We don't but we have a big kitchen. Mammy wants to buy a range when she has the money."

"We have a range."

"I know, Mammy cleans it out on Fridays."

"Where did your Mammy make the cake for us?" I wondered.

"In the pot on the grille."

It being the same way Nanny Ward made her cakes, made me think of the nannas. I was working out in my head when I could go to see them as Maura was saying, "We have a back kitchen with a sink and another tap in the toilet, so we can wash our hands and face."

It was smashing with Maura telling me about her house. Sometimes my feet slid on the crispy road, but I didn't fall because Maura was holding my hand. Maura brought me to the door of my school. Before she left to go to her own school, which was the Mercy Convent further along the Cork Road, she told me to wait inside the door until she came for me.

It was funny being in school again. I hung my coat up in the cloakroom and crept into my desk keeping my eyes lowered. Sister Ignatius was at her table looking towards the door on the bad side because the children from the Home were filing in. I looked too. Brigid was there, shining and quivering with cold like the frost on leaves. I didn't see Liam, so I supposed he still had the measles and wasn't out of the woods yet and the doctor wouldn't let him back for another good while. Loretta wasn't in her seat and I wondered if she had the measles.

We didn't look at the cat on the mat in the first pages of the reading book but went to see a boy and a toy on page twelve. In catechism class we were learning about the Holy Ghost, who was everywhere but you didn't see him. I wanted to know about him in case he was a cousin of the Coster Bower. I didn't fidget but I think he was only the son of God and the brother of Jesus and the three of them were stuck together.

We put on our coats before we went out to the yard. I rushed over to Úna and Kait. They asked me if I was better and I asked them about Ducking Night.

"Arlene, it was great *spraoi*."

"It was, so it was."

"I blackened my face with soot and put my cardigan on inside out and Kait wore one of her mother's old dresses."

"I did, so I did, and our lanterns were smashing. Úna's baby brother got frightened when he looked out the door and saw all the scary eyes and mouths swimming along."

"The street was jammed with everybody carrying lanterns and poor Brendan nearly jumped out his skin when he saw the lit-up faces in the dark."

"We had to show him our turnip with the candle inside, so he knew it was only us."

"Did ye get any pennies?"

"No but we got five halfpennies between us."

"Ye did?"

"We did but that auld, stupid pig Mr Delaney said we were using Ducking Night to beg and ran us away."

"I told my big brother, and he got the mean yoke back."

"What did he do?"

"He stooped down and crept up to Delaney's door and tied a piece of fishing gut to the knocker."

"What for?"

"To pull it and knock on his door."

"But he'd see your brother when he opened the door."

"No, silly goose, they ran and hid behind the hedge outside his railing and he couldn't see them in the dark."

"It was great *spraoi* to see him opening the door and nobody there."

"We pulled the string a few times and then cleared off when he came out with his dogs."

"He was going to set his dogs on us, so he was."

"He's awful, so next Ducking Night we will do plenty of door slamming to madden him."

"I betcha even the spirits don't come back to visit Mr Delaney's house, so they didn't."

"Did ye get any sweets?"

"We didn't but we got barm breac and hazelnuts from plenty of people."

"That's cos the big boys go to Castle Hackett woods and get nuts, so they do," Kait explained.

"My brother went as well, cos he wanted to see the woods near Cnoc Maa," Úna said proudly.

"Did he put salt in his pocket?" Kait wanted to know.

I was wondering why they had to put salt in their pockets and asked, "What for?"

"That's why," Kait said cos she didn't know why.

Úna, who was big, knew and told me, "So the fairies don't take you away with them."

"Do they not like salt?" I asked surprised.

"I don't know," Úna answered.

Kait tried to show off she knew everything, saying, "If you don't have salt in your pocket, they'll take you away because Queen Maeve lives in Cnoc Maa."

"I know she does cos Mrs McLoughlin told me," I answered, putting my face up near hers to show her she wasn't the boss of me.

She didn't know how to answer and only said, "Nan and Nanny said you are to come to see them, so you are."

"I will when I can. Tell Prince I was asking for him."

Lent

Maura was waiting for me and I was glad because it was still half black in the street. I caught her hand and held on to it. "Maura, are you going to come for me every day now?"

"Only for a while. Mammy got me a job in Wynn's shop and I'm starting on St Brigid's Day.

"You're too small to work in a shop."

"I'm working upstairs in the house minding the children. In no time the evenings will start getting bright and you can go home on your own."

"I can cos I'm big. When is St Brigid's Day?"

"Very soon and after that it's St Patrick's day."

"What is St Patrick's Day, Maura?" I asked. She told me we had no school that day and we could eat all the sweets we liked. I was surprised people couldn't eat sweets the other days and said, "I can eat sweets all the time."

"Because you're small but when you make your First Holy Communion, you get big and do things the big people do."

"What do they do?"

"The nuns will tell you all about it so don't be asking me questions like Catherine and Jim are always doing."

"Alright, I won't," I said real quick, so she wouldn't get vexed.

Maura was right. One day after school when I went out to the street it wasn't dark. As the days got longer, I started coming home on my own and after tea, going out to play with my pals. As the evenings were getting brighter, everyone was getting happier and talking about stretch in the evening, but John Delaney was a silly goose saying, "It won't be long until Ash Wednesday is on us and we're wearing the ashes on our foreheads."

I asked Daddy about the ashes because he smokes and would know.

"Arlene, the only thing you and I will be doing on Shrove Tuesday is eating pancakes."

"I know, Daddy. Everyone in Drumbron has pancakes for tea."

At school, Úna and Kait were saying they were dying for Pancake Tuesday to come so they could stuff themselves with pancakes.

On Ash Wednesday, Mammy went to Mass with Mr Delaney and came home with her forehead dirty because the priest had pressed a cork against it and left a dirty spot that was supposed to be a cross.

At school Sr Ignatius didn't talk about pancakes, only about the forty days of Lent. It was when people didn't eat meat on Fridays, and they did penance for their sins. There were lots of sins. They had different names to be able to tell the priest about them in confession. Before, no one knew the names of the sins, so God wrote ten commandments on two big stone slates and gave them to a man called Moses. The commandments were things you could not do and if you did any of those things written on the stones, you had committed a sin. We were learning the commandments off by heart so we wouldn't break them and commit a sin. The fourth one was very important, "Thou shalt love and honour thy parents." It only meant we had to be good and not give cheek to our mammies and daddies.

Daddy, Mammy and Mr Delaney were in the kitchen talking about Lent. Mammy had given up sweets and sugar. Mr Delaney wasn't going to eat any more biscuits. Daddy didn't say anything, so I asked him, "Daddy, are you giving up smoking?"

"I amn't but John is giving up Chester cake."

Mammy gave Daddy a vexed look and Mr Delaney opened his eyes wide and said nothing. Later on, when he got up to leave, he said, "It won't be long until Easter is on us and we're eating the eggs."

Daddy answered, "Aye but we'll have St Patricks first."

Mr Delaney was always in our house and that's why I asked Mammy if he was a relative and part of our family.

"Whatever put that into your head? Of course he isn't, he's Daddy's friend."

I was surprised because Mr Delaney seemed more like Mammy's friend with the way he was always talking with her, nearly like an old woman. Daddy liked to go to the parish hall to play cards and talk about the game and the beef factory with Dr Kelly, while Mammy and Mr Delaney were always talking about girls going to their aunts.

"Dervla, that Kelly one's mother is saying the daughter is off to England to stay with her aunt."

"I'm not surprised, she was a wild one," Mammy would answer nodding her head and looking cross.

"Her aunt, *mar dhea*. There's too many like that Kelly one around."

"There is indeed."

The two of them used to get cross about girls going to their aunts in England. I suppose Mammy liked him because he helped her choose the new curtains and carpets for the sitting room and always went to Sligo or Galway when she needed to buy new clothes. I hated the guts out of him but there was one good thing about him – when my mother was talking to him in the parlour, she didn't notice that I went out to play with my pals. As soon as I ate my bread and butter with the sliced hard-boiled egg or ham, I went to the nannas low thatched cottages on Clonthu Hill but didn't bother telling Mammy.

In my mother's mind some people were above her, like Mrs Fitzgerald and others were beneath her, like my pals. I knew that because one day when I wanted to sit on the same side of the chapel as Úna, Mammy put a vexed look on her face and told me we couldn't sit with those rough and ignorant people. I never told her about my pals Úna and Kait and besides, Daddy used to say it was better not to tell her certain things, so as not to vex her. I didn't bother telling her about the nannas so as not to vex her. But she was a silly goose because the nannas were smashing altogether.

When the Nannas walked, moving their long skirts that reached down to the tops of their boots, like the boats that I saw gliding across the harbour when Mammy, Daddy and me were in Trafada. The bright shawl with different coloured squares that Nanny Ward threw across her shoulders and covered her head when it rained, was nicer than the coats Mammy wore. Nanny had a red petticoat that showed under her black skirt and looked lovely. Nan Gormley was different and dressed all in black.

"Nan, why don't you have a colourful shawl too?"

"When Jack died, my heart was broken, and all the colour went out of my life. How could I be going around in cheerful clothes and him in the grave."

"*Tráth*, tell the child the real reason. The shawl went to pawn-shop to pay for the wake."

"Well, there is a bit of truth in that now."

"A girleen, the women's shawls are the first thing to go when money was needed."

"For wakes?"

"For everything. During the times of the Big Hunger my mother said it was the shawls that always went first to pay the rent or buy a drop of stir-about."

"What was the Big Hunger, Nanny?"

"*Tráth*, it was an awful time altogether. Sure, weren't the people dying on the side of the road and their mouths green from eating the grass," Nan said.

Nanny blessed herself as she added, "Ne'er a prayer said for them or a shaking of holy water over their dead bodies."

"Was the Big Hunger in Drumbron, Nan?"

"Indeedin it was. My own mother said people with only the flesh covering their bones came from every corner of the county to Drumbron."

"An awful sight to see with eyes as big as the full moon shinning in their shrunken heads," Nanny added.

"Why they did they come to our town, Nanny?"

"If ya had money you could buy the yalla meal or if you hadn't, you'd go to the workhouse up the Cork Road."

"It was many the one from my own place of Suilín Beag that dragged themselves into Drumbron," Nan said in a *brónach* voice.

"The workhouse wasn't big enough to hold all that wanted to get in. Sure, weren't the people dying on their feet."

"Why were they dying on their feet?"

"When they went to the gate and weren't let in, the only thing left for them to do was die."

"My own place of Suilín Beag is gone. If you went along the road by the Suilín River, sure you'd never know there was a village out there at all."

"Where is it gone to, Nan?"

"The earth swallowed the houses up with the people dead inside them."

"Why was that, Nan?

"*A grá*, the hungry brought sickness on them and made them weak and all they could do was die to get away from the suffering that was on them."

"Who buried them?"

"No one buried them. The houses became the graves."

"When I was young, we used to bless ourselves when we passed by our tumbled down houses," Nanny said.

"Why Nanny?"

"Some of my people were in the ground and no headstone to mark the spot where they were lying," Nanny said and blessed herself again.

Nan gave her a look and mouthed, "*Ná béid ag caint.*" and then asked, "Which of ye three young craturs will go out and get water from the pump?"

We pushed each other trying to be the first to take the jug down from the dresser but Úna got it. When we came back, the nannas were saying prayers in Irish. I suppose it was for Nanny's family who were under the ground. After we had tea, we ran outside to play *Buille*. Liam's face was in my head, so I told Úna and Kait I wanted to go to the gable-end of the house the nannas said was from the Big Hunger time. I blessed myself and said a Hail Mary and told the people lying underneath it that I was sorry they died, because they had no food to eat and told them I was going to put some Marietta biscuits under my pillow for Liam.

At school the next day, I tripped on my way out to the yard and pushed the biscuit in under Brigid's desk. She looked up but I think her soul was with the fairies because her eyes were hollow. Liam was a good while sick. I crossed my fingers for him to get better and come back to school to learn about sins so he could make his first confession.

At home Mammy was putting the last touches to my communion dress. She told me I needed white shoes, ankle socks, a veil and white gloves too. As well as all those, I needed a white bag to put my new rosary beads in. Mr Delaney was drinking tea and said he would drive us to Sligo as there was more shops there and then the silly goose said to me, "It won't be long until your Communion Day is on us, Mary."

In Sligo, the *amadán* told everyone, "It won't be long until Easter is on us and we are eating the eggs." But he wasn't right because we had Palm Sunday before Easter Sunday and everyone got branches at Mass. Mammy told me it was to remember the day Jesus rode through a city called Jerusalem on an ass and people cheered and waved palm branches. Good Friday was another day everyone spoke about. It was a sad because Jesus was crucified on the cross. He was put into the tomb and stayed there until Easter Sunday when he rose again.

On Easter Sunday, the day Jesus, came back from the dead, people wore something new to show they were happy he was alive. Mammy bought me a light blue cardigan in McCabe's clothes shop to wear to Mass. Úna and Kait were in the side aisle wearing new ribbons in their hair. I don't know what Brigid or Liam got new because we had holidays and didn't have school. That Sunday everyone tried to eat as many eggs as their tummies would let them. My tummy was small and after eating two and a half eggs, I couldn't eat any more. Daddy said he ate five, but his eggs were scrambled so I didn't know how many Mammy had broken into the saucepan with the butter and milk. In the evening time when Mr Delaney came, he told us he had duck eggs because they were bigger.

"What colour are duck eggs?" I asked.

"Look at your cardigan, it's duck-egg-blue," Mammy said. After that I didn't like my new cardigan much because it reminded me of Mr Delaney stuffing his mouth with duck eggs.

After the holidays, we started back in school with Sr Ignatius jumpy and shouting at everyone, except Loretta and her pals, because the priest was coming in the following day to examine us for our First Holy Communion. Fr Mannion was the priest's name and he asked easy questions and when some children got nervous and didn't answer right, he half told them the answer, so in the end we all passed. That meant we could go to the church on Friday to make our first confession and get our souls cleaned to receive Holy Jesus into our souls. Before Fr Mannion left, he told us our First Holy Communion would be the happiest day of our lives.

As soon as school was over, we rushed up Clonthu Hill to tell the nannas we had passed our catechism exam. They knew we were coming and had crubeens and cabbage boiled because we loved sucking the crubeens and eating the jelly-meat around the bones. Nanny peeled the spuds and dropped them on our plates with plenty of butter while we told them what question the priest had asked us. They laughed when we told them about Loretta.

"Loretta, my dear child, how many persons are there in the Holy Trinity?"

"Seven, Father."

"Loretta, you know there are THREE persons in the Holy Trinity."

"Yes, Father."

"They are the Father, the Son and…"

"The daughter, Father."

"The Holy Ghost is the third one, as you well know, Loretta."

"Yes, Father."

When we were finished eating, Nan took out the pouch she had tied around her neck with the string like shoe lacers. It was hidden under her jumper in the spot between her diddies. It was full of the coins she was saving for her wake.

Taking a coin out for each of us, she said to make sure to come and show her our dresses and veils. Her and Nanny told us that our First Holy Communion Day was the happiest day of our lives.

The Best Day of my Life

Our First Confession on Friday was smashing. We made a line of twos and went out of school and into the street. Sr Ignatius, at the very top of the line, was holding no one's hand. Behind her was Loretta holding Regina Burke's hand, behind them was me holding Noeleen Pitt's hand. Pauline Byrne and Fionnuala McCabe came next. Úna and Kait were at the back with the children from the bad side. Sr Paul, holding no one's hand was at the very end. The Home Babies didn't come because they had their own chapel in the Home.

We went in the side door to the small aisle in the part of the chapel with the pictures on the wall of Jesus carrying the cross, and where Úna and Kait sit for Mass. The nun led us passed two wooden boxes stuck into the bench on the wall, to the last bench and box up at the very end where the statue of Our Lady was. The nun said this was the confessional box we were going into. We were to sit on the bench and be very quiet.

Sr Ignatius opened one of the two doors on each side of the dark confessional box and Sr Paul opened the other. Our nun took Loretta by the hand and brought her to the door. Loretta went in. Sr Paul was holding Regina's hand on the other side. She went into the other one. We waited wondering where they had gone, and would they come out again They did come out and knelt down on the long seats in front of the statue of Our Lady. Then it was my turn and Noeleen's turn to go in through the doors.

The wooden box was like a coffin standing up and I was frightened but pretended I wasn't. Sr Ignatius told me to kneel on the little step under a funny window with a curtain. She closed the door, and the tiny room became dark. I bit the back of my hand and wanted to do wee-wee because I heard voices whispering and mumbling inside the funny window. I nearly screamed when the curtain opened. I saw white teeth moving behind the criss-cross boards. My mouth wouldn't open to say, "Bless me Father, for I have sinned." but I remembered I was supposed to say it was my first confession when the teeth asked, "How long since your last confession, my child." I told him all my sins. He told me to say a prayer for penance and to go in peace and he shut the window with a snap. My first confession was finished, and I stood up as Sr Ignatius opened the door and pulled me out by the shoulder and told me to kneel and say my penance.

It took me ages to remember a prayer and then I said, "God bless Mammy and Daddy." like I say at the end of my prayers as night. Everyone else had their hands joined, their heads bowed, and their mouths mumbling like me.

On Saturday, Mammy got me up when Daddy was having his breakfast. She told me not to dress but to come downstairs in my nightdress. We had a lot to do because tomorrow was my First Holy Communion Day.

"William, fill up the bath before you go to the barracks and put some more turf on the fire," said Mammy.

Daddy picked up the kettle and poured it into the tin bath in front of the fire and emptied the two big pots boiling on the range into it as well. "Arlene, you're going to be spotless for tomorrow," he said as he lifted me into the bath. Then he was saying goodbye and rushing out the door. Mammy washed and dressed me real quick.

"The whole town will be getting their hair set today, so we better hurry."

"How do you get your set? Is it like the jelly?"

"Whist. Grab that piece of bread and butter and eat it on the way uptown."

In Peggy's hairdresser's there were five chairs against the wall with people sitting on all of them, while children were standing, leaning against their mammies, like me. When the hairdresser saw Mammy coming in the door, she hurried over holding a comb and a fat sausage thing in her hand. Bending close to my mother's face she whispered something. Mammy smiled saying, "That's very good of you, Peggy."

An older woman who was looking at us said, "Mrs Blake, have my chair."

"No, not at all, I'm fine."

"Sure, it will do me legs good to stretch them a bit."

"I couldn't."

"Here you are, Mrs Blake. Sure, what would I be doing with me sitting down and you standing up," the woman said as she stepped to the side of the chair. Mammy nodded her thanks and sat down. She picked up a magazine and started looking at it, instead of talking to the woman who had given her the chair. Peggy, the hairdresser, finished putting the fat sausage things in the hair of the woman she had sitting on a chair.

"Mammy, what is Peggy doing to the woman's hair?"

"She is putting in rollers."

Peggy put a hairnet around the hair and led the rolled woman to another seat with a sort of wide lamp that was hanging on a metal bar.

"What's that, Mammy?"

"It's a hairdryer but Mary, remember what I told you about being seen, not heard."

"Alright, Mammy."

Peggy called Mammy over to a basin stuck to the wall covered with a big mirror and put a towel around her shoulders. After washing my mother's hair, Peggy picked up a comb with a long tail and used it to make a short line on the top of Mammy's head. Then she took a pink roller thing, from a box with trays, and twisted that piece of hair around the pink roller and stuck a hair pin into it. Peggy did the same to every bit of hair on Mammy's head. Then she asked Mammy to sit in a different seat and put her head under the hairdryer.

Mammy had her hair cut to her chin, like a woman called Jackie Kennedy who was always in the magazines.

She and Mr Delaney went to Sligo to buy a suit for my communion like the ones Jackie wore. My hair was long, down my back, not short like Mammy's. I didn't want Peggy sticking my head into that basin on the wall and drowning me with water, so I moved behind the woman, who had given Mammy the chair, and looked at the floor. I crossed my fingers hoping Peggy wouldn't see me in my hiding place.

I nearly jumped out of my skin when I heard her say, "Mary, can you come over with me to the wash basin."

She had put two cushions on the seat to make me taller. She washed my hair and rubbed my head real hard with a towel. I wanted to cry but knew Mammy would be annoyed with me for disgracing her, so I put my knuckles into my mouth. I bit them when Peggy combed out the tangles with quick movements that pulled the skin on my head and made me wince. While she was pulling and dragging my hair, she said, "I heard you were sick. How are you now?"

"Better than yourself," I said like the man in the hotel had said to Mr Delaney the day I had the trifle.

"Mary, how dare you answer like that," Mammy said in a cross voice from under the lamp. When the old man said the same thing to Mr Delaney in the Royal Hotel, she had smiled.

"Mrs Blake, I won't use the rollers. I'll just brush Mary's hair into curls."

"Do that, Peggy."

My head was hurting but I kept quiet because Mammy's eyes left the magazine every now and then to dart over to me. I knew I had to be good and not complain. I started thinking about how Loretta got ringlets put in her hair every night to look like Shirley Temple. It's stupid to hurt yourself to look nice. I was glad when Peggy finished with my hair.

The hair dryer Mammy was under made a click sound. Peggy lifted half the front and Mammy came out. She sat on a chair in front of a mirror while Peggy pulled the rollers from Mammy's hair.

"I'll backcomb this bit on top." She made piles of tangles with the comb and then brushed a piece that had no tangles over it and sprayed lacquer on the two sides, the back and front of Mammy's hair. When we left the place, I thought we were going to *An Lár*, but Mammy said we had to go home so the wind wouldn't ruin our hair.

At home, when I touched my Mammy's hair, it was stiff like a board, but Mammy was happy and smiling. Later when Mr Delaney came to visit, he helped her put on the pink, pillar-box hat they had bought in Sligo at the back of her head. She looked beautiful.

At teatime, Mammy told me to eat plenty.

"Do I have to fill myself to the brink?"

"You do because after tea you can't eat anything else."

"Why? That's not fair."

"Because to receive, you fast all night and morning."

"Receive what, Mammy?"

"Your First Holy Communion, of course."

Daddy winked at me and said, "You're a big girl now and have to do what the grown-ups do, so you'll have to piggyback me upstairs to bed."

"I can't, Daddy, you're too heavy."

Before I went to bed, Mammy put a hairnet around my ringlets so they wouldn't fall out during the night. Daddy laughed. He said his mother used to wear a hairnet too, to keep the bun on her head in place.

"Why did Granny Arlene put the bun on her head instead of eating it?"

"Mary, a bun is what the old women called their hairstyle."

"Like Nanny Ward's at the back of her head."

"Who's Nanny Ward?"

"A woman who goes into Byrne's Sweetshop," I said thinking I would have to tell the priest in confession that I had told a lie.

My First Holy Communion

My communion day was smashing. A crown of white flowers with shiny beads in the middle, kept my veil on. I wore white gloves and carried a bag. Daddy even came to the Mass to watch me walk in with all the boys and girls from our school. The children from the other school sat in the opposite benches to us. The Home Babies didn't come because they had their own chapel in the Home and were making their communion there.

Everyone was buzzing as happy as a bumblebee except Loretta. Sr Ignatius had to give her a drink of water. She was feeling faint because she hadn't eaten her sliced pan bread with no crusts. I didn't care I had no breakfast. Úna and Kait told me their big sisters and brothers told them after we made our First Holy Communion, we were having a feast in the convent parlour.

We stood up when Sr Ignatius and Sr Paul stood up and sat down or knelt when they did. Then after a long time, we were sliding out of our seats and going up to the railings to receive. The priest stood in front of me with a big, golden glass, with one leg like the trifle glass. He lifted a round thin wafer from it. I stuck out my tongue at him and he placed the Host on it. Jesus didn't taste of anything and was hard to swallow. After making plenty of spit in my mouth, He went down my throat. I stood up, put my hands with my lovely white gloves under my chin, lowered my head and walked back to my place. I thanked God for coming into my soul with the prayer we had learned. This was the happiest day of my life.

Straight after Mass, Loretta, Noeleen and Regina were left with their parents because they were going to the bishop's palace. All the rest of us stayed. Daddy kissed me and said I looked like a little angel.

The nuns led us back to the convent, to the part where the nuns lived. We went up the steps through the wide-open door, across a delph floor with beautiful drawings in it and into the parlour. There was a long table with a white tablecloth full of cups and plates, glasses and spoons. Sr Ignatius and Sr Paul showed us where to sit. Then a pile of nuns fluttered out from a door at the end of the room. A few carried big kettles with two handles, one in front of the lid and the other behind. While the teapot nuns poured tea into our cups, the others put milk and sugar into them. Other nuns were handing us ham sandwiches and slices of bread and butter. After we had eaten our breakfast, the nuns came back with jelly and custard and lemonade in big jugs. They placed cakes and biscuits on the table and told us to help ourselves.

The cake I liked the best was long one, like a big, fat sausage. It had jam and cream in the creases that went round and round. When the nun cut it into slices she asked, "Who would like a slice of swiss roll?" We all put up our hands.

While we were at the feast, the nuns kept wiping our faces because we had to be clean for the photos. Then we went out to the garden and stood on the steps outside the convent door. Sr Ignatius said it was the class photo and we had to stand in a group. She put me in the back row because I was tall. Úna was in the middle and Kait in the front. After the class photo, we stood in a line waiting to get our photo taken by ourselves. I was talking to Úna saying how smashing the feast was when the woman who was helping the man with the camera, called my name. She led me to stand in front of him, telling me to smile and to join my hands in front of me with my white rosary beads dangling down. He clicked the box he was holding.

Then Mammy and Daddy appeared, and we went home. On the way back, anyone we met stopped us and said I looked beautiful and my First Holy Communion day was the happiest day of my life.

Mrs McLoughlin made the dinner for us and brought the roast chicken to our house for us. I couldn't eat any. Mammy opened a tin box of biscuits, like at Christmas time, for all the people who kept calling in all day. They patted me on the head and put half crowns and shillings into my hand. Mr Delaney gave me a pound note. Mammy took all the money and said we would open an account in the post office. It was nice being the star, as Daddy said, and having everyone want to see me on the happiest day of my life, but what I really wanted to do was to go up Clonthu Hill to show the nannas my dress, as I had promised.

That night in bed when I looked over at Will in the picture on the mantlepiece, I wondered if Liam in the Home liked the swiss roll and if the lemonade had made his nose go fizzy.

Úna didn't come to school the day after our First Holy Communion. Kait told me she had stuffed herself with too many sweets and her tummy was sick. Liam and Brigid weren't in class either. I supposed their tummies were hurting them from eating too many sweets.

That evening I went to see the nannas to say I was sorry for not showing them my dress. Úna was there with her nanna, Nan Gormley. Before I opened my mouth, Nan took the pouch out and put a sixpence into my hand.

"Nan, I can't take it."

"And why is that, a girleen?"

"I promised I would show you my dress and I didn't come here yesterday."

"Arlene, sure you're only a child. You do what you're told to do."

"But Nan…"

"Don't worry, a child. Now if I didn't keep my word, I would have to come back from the next world, like poor auld March Lydon."

"What happened to March, Nan?"

"Ah, a girleen, it's like this. Marcheen needed a few shillings to pay the train and boat fare and he asked Molly for it."

"He did indeed, *a stóirín,* and said 'Molly, as sure as God in that picture there on the wall,' he said pointing to the Sacred Heart, 'when I come back from Scotland, I'll pay every penny I owe you,'" said Nanny Ward.

"Why did he go to Scotland, Nanny?"

"To pick the praties."

"My daddy goes to pick praties too and he brings Mammy back money," Kait said.

"To cut a long story short, wasn't I sitting up in the bed one night saying my rosary when there was three loud knocks on the window," Nanny Ward said.

"Who was knocking, Nanny?"

"No one because when I drew back the curtains, there wasn't a sinner outside."

"There wasn't?"

"There wasn't but when I picked up my beads and started the decade of the sorrowful, I heard the three knocks again."

"What did you do?"

"I put my hand under the pillow and took out the bottle of Knock holy water I have there and sprinkled some on the window and cried out, 'In the name of God, I command you to make yourself known.'"

Me and Kait were up on top of each other with our fists in our mouths and shaking with fright.

"Nan what happened?"

"The face of March appeared."

"Was he back from Scotland?"

"The very thoughts crossed my mind, a girl. I said 'Will ya come in or that, March and don't be frightening the life out of me.'"

"What did he say?" This time it was Kait who asked the question.

"The voice that came out of his mouth made the air around me go cold."

"It said, 'Molly, in the name of God and all his saints, I beseech you to help me!'"

"'March, if there is anything I can do, I'll do it, *a mhic*,' I said to him and meaning every word of what I said."

"Only you can give my soul the rest it needs," he answered in the voice that was putting the heart cross ways in me. "Marcheen, for the love of God, tell me what you want?"

"Release me from the promise I made you, I implore you from the depths of my soul," he begged.

"And what promise would that be now, *a mhic*, sure it's many the promise you made."

"Molly, if there is any pity in your heart, you will pardon me the fare," he said.

At that moment Nan realised there was a red glow around the face looking at her through the windowpane, so she asked, "What fare would that be now, *a mhic*?" wondering if what he was smoking in his pipe was causing the red glow in the dark night.

"The train and boat fare. Before I left, I swore under the image of Christ Himself I would pay you back."

"Indeedin you did, but as I said to Mary Gormley the very same day you left, I said and she heard me say it, 'When my Pakie died, the lad couldn't do enough for me and there is no money in this world to repay him the kindness he showed me. You owe me nothing, a Marcheen, *a stóirín*."

"Molly, say you release me from my debt."

"I do, I release you from your debt. There is not a penny owing to me from you."

"My blessing on you, Molly. I can go on my way."

"Indeed, you can and if there is anything owing, it's on my side, March."

"The blessings of God, His holy Mother and the saints on you, Molly."

"Will ya come in out of the night and not be talking to me through the window," I told him, but he said he had a long journey to make and was gone like he came.

Nan Gormley continued telling us the rest of the story. "Every word Molly is telling ye is as true as sure as there's a God in heaven. Sure, the sun wasn't up for long the next morning when Molly was standing where you are now, a girleen, telling me how Martin had asked her to pardon him the money he owed her."

"Why didn't he want to pay."

"He wanted to pay but he couldn't because he was dead."

"Dead!" I echoed. Kait grabbed me by the arm and sunk her fingers into my flesh.

"It was his ghost who was talking to Molly that night."

Kait was squeezing my arm tight, like Mammy does to the lemon to get the last drop of juice out. I asked in a shaky voice, "How did ye know he was dead?"

"A telegram that broke our hearts, came the next day. Poor March was with his Maker."

"If he was with his Maker, he wasn't dead," I said puzzled.

But Kait who was big and knew everything said, "His Maker means Holy God, so he was in Heaven, cos God only lets dead people into heaven."

I shook her hand off me and asked the nannas how he got dead.

"How did he die, Nanny?"

"Not a death you would wish on anyone."

I said, "What happened?"

"It wasn't til the others came back from the pratie picking that we heard the sad news."

"What did they tell ye?"

"A sad story. When they got off the boat, sick and weary, they waited for the train they were taking them to Ayrshire."

"Why did they wait?" I asked. Kait was silent without asking any questions, maybe because she knew the story cos her daddy went pratie-picking to Scotland for money.

"On account of the train not leaving until the early hours of the morning."

"Where did they wait?"

"The night was spent in the station in Glasgow but Mart, wanting to stretch his legs, took into his head to go for a walk on his own."

"Wasn't it night-time, Nanny, and dark?"

"Right in the middle of the night and that notion to take a walk was the death of him."

"How's that?"

"He bumped into a bad crowd. And nothing less than beat the life out of him, is what they did."

"Why would they do that?"

"There's a queer lot there in Glasgow who hate the sight of the Irish." Then looking at Kait's worried face, she said quickly, "It doesn't happen now, it's a mighty long time since Marteen went tattie hawking."

"But when Marteen died, he couldn't keep his promise and pay me."

"Sure, you didn't mind if he didn't, did you?"

"I didn't but as he forgot to say *Le Cuige Dé*, he had to come back."

"What's *Le Cuige Dé*?"

"With the help of God. When people make a promise and say, 'With the help of God' it doesn't matter if they can't keep the promise."

I knew two prayers to keep me from harm. The Act of Contrition so I wouldn't fall into the burning fires of hell and 'With the help of God' to keep my spirit in the next world if I couldn't keep a promise.

When I went home Mr Delaney was eating Daddy's Chester cake and telling Mammy Cathal McHugh was down at the Parochial House, legless at usual and cursing at the priest, so he was signed into Ballinacora. I wondered if there was a special prayer Cathal could say to save himself from them locking him up.

Mammy was beating eggs in a bowl and adding warm milk to it because Mr Delaney had shown her how to make French Toast. It is lovely soft bread with sugar on top, but I was getting sick of it because we were having it nearly every evening for tea. When he was leaving, he said, "We'll never feel until the Bonfire Night and the longest day in the year is on us."

The days were longer because the sun was staying and not going home until late, and we were able to play outside in the street until the stars came out.

One evening, when I was coming back from playing, Daddy was in the back garden.

"What are you doing, Daddy?"

"Look at the night sky."

"I want to see it."

He lifted me up, took my sandals off and put me standing on his shoulders.

"Arlene, reach up to the sky and touch the stars."

"What stars, Daddy?"

"The Plough."

I tried to but it was up real high. "I can't, Daddy. They are too far up."

"Aye, the land is flat in this part of the country. We'll go to the Culliagh mountains, near my place, and see if you can reach up higher."

"When, Daddy, when?"

"One of these days, when you have school holidays, Missy."

"Alright, Daddy, but that will be soon because it's summer. Look, I have my sandals and ankle socks on, and Mammy doesn't tell me to wear my *geansaí* or cardigan in the morning."

"Aye, it is weather for summer clothes."

"Daddy, some girls in my class wear white shoes with tongues but no lacers. Do you know they are called sand shoes?" I was thinking of Úna and Kait, who stopped wearing boots a good while after our communion, but the Home Babies still had their boots on.

"Aye, the cloth is canvas, good for this fine weather."

The nice weather was making Sr Ignatius nice too. Every day when we came back from the yard and did a few sums, we made a line to go to Castle Fields.

The Home Babies made a different line and went to the Home. They weren't in Sports Day because they had no mammies and daddies to come and see them on the last day of class.

"Loretta, do you want to hold Regina or Noeleen's hand in the line?" the nun asked Miss Special as she directed the rest of the class to stand in a line holding another child's hand. "I want to hold the two of their hands, Sister."

"Alright, Loretta," Sr Ignatius let the three of them stand together at the top of the line with Loretta in the middle, holding the other two other girls hands.

"You, Mary Blake, stand beside Evelyn Curry."

Evelyn Curry was one of the girls who sat on the good side. Her wiry hair was a brown, foxy colour and her eyes were too, with her face full of freckles. She reminded me of Mr Delaney's fox-terrier dog.

We followed Sr Ignatius through the convent gardens to the Castle Fields with Sister Paul walking at the end of the line.

In the green field, where the big girls played camogie, we practiced the races for Sports Day. We pretended we were holding up a sack and jumped instead of running for the sack-race.

For the egg and spoon race, we ran holding one hand out in front. We were supposed to hold a spoon with an egg balanced on it. On the real Sports Day, we would get the egg and spoon, the nun said.

Sister Paul tied one of my legs to one of Evelyn's for the one-legged race. Sr Ignatius blew the whistle. We half ran, half jumped to the finishing line, which was the goal post. Every time we stumbled Evelyn held onto me and told me not to fall. She didn't want us to be like Loretta and her pals. They kept tumbling to the ground and weren't able to get up until Sister Ignatius helped them.

"Don't fall, Mary, hold on to me," she said.

I grabbed her around the waist and trying not to laugh said, "Shut up laughing cos you are shaking and making me wobbly and that's why I'm falling."

We had great *spraoi*. Before we went home, I brought her over to my pals. They were talking about bonfire night. She asked Úna if she could come to the Kilmartin Bonfire cos she lived on Sligo Road. Úna said she would have to help gather stuff for the fire if she wanted to be part of the gang and I told her she had to call me Arlene and not Mary if she wanted to come to the bonfire.

The next day in the yard, Evelyn planned with us how we would go gathering tyres, rags, old newspapers and anything that burned for the fire. After tea I sloped out of my house when Mammy was talking to Batt, the postman, and met my pals at the station. Úna had the pram because she had to mind her little brother and baby sister.

"Can your sister walk, Úna?" Evelyn asked.

"She can. Teresa started walking last year and Brendan knows well how to walk," Úna said showing off about them.

"When we get the things for the bonfire, we'll put them in the pram and the children can walk," Evelyn said taking charge.

"I don't know about that!" Úna was used to me and Kait doing what she told us to do and she didn't like Evelyn being the boss. "Teresa's legs are small. She gets tired quick."

"Well, we can take turns carrying her, Úna," Evelyn said.

"I can give Teresa a piggyback, so I can," said Kait.

"So can I," I said really quick after Kait.

"Alright. Let's go to the sawmills first to see if they have any blocks," Úna said.

Evelyn added, "We'll ask the man for a bag of sawdust too."

Me and Kait walked together, say nothing and every now and then we looked at the other two. Úna was used to planning everything for our gang but now she had Evelyn to help her.

We heard Úna boasting to Evelyn she was going to jump over the fire. "My big brother always takes a running jump and leaps over the fire and never gets burned, so I'm going to jump over it too."

"My brother jumps it too, so he does."

"Mrs McLoughlin said Jock Connors plays and people dance and sing, so I'm not getting sick this time and going for sure," I said. remembering how I had missed out on Ducking Night.

"You never said 'With the help of God.' so you didn't," Kait scolded, so straight away I said the magic words, "With the help Of God."

From the bike's shop, we got an old bicycle tyre that had more patches on it than rubber. We put it in beside Teresa. She put her hands around it and brought it to her mouth and started sucking it. Úna told her to stop but she wouldn't, so we took the baby out and Kait carried her on her back.

Kait was smaller than me and Úna. She looked light and airy like a feather, but she was plucky. That was the word Daddy used for the lads he trained when they played a good game of football.

"Where do we keep the stuff we gather?" Evelyn wanted to know as she picked up a log from the side of the road.

"In Nanny Ward's and she'll give us tea too when we go up Clonthu Road."

"I'm going home now and can't go with ye."

"Why?"

"Cos my Daddy will be home from the barracks for tea."

"Is your Daddy a Garda too?" Úna and Kait said at the same time with round mouths and eyes.

"He is," Evelyn said and skipped off, running as fast as a greyhound.

Our bonfire was going to be in the middle of three roads, on the space where St Jarlath's Avenue, Clonthu Hill and Kilmartin Road meet. Kevin, Tom, Seán and their gang would be with us because they lived in St Jarlath's Terrace. Evelyn lived in Sligo Road. Úna wasn't from our part of town, but she was the one who was in charge of the bonfire. She said she might go to her own one near Dun na Rí Road and Cork Road when she got tired of our one.

On bonfire night, Mammy put me to bed at the same time as always. I pretended I was tired, but my body was trembling, thinking about being out in the navy-blue night and seeing the glow of the fire. I waited until Mammy was in the parlour for a long, long time. I knew she sat on the sofa talking to Mr Delaney about Princess Margaret and Jackie Kennedy who were in the magazines she read. After ages I put my dress and shoes on and sloped downstairs. The door didn't budge when I pulled it back. It was locked. I stood on my tiptoes and stretched myself up, wanting to turn the tiny, brass knob on the lock at the top of the door. I had seen Mammy do it with her thumb and finger, but I couldn't reach it. I was mad and wanted to kick the door and scream. I thought of going to the kitchen for a chair but was afraid Mammy would see me passing by as the radio was on low in the parlour. I kept reaching up my hand, but I couldn't open the door. In the end I went back upstairs to the landing.

From the window at the side of it, I looked at the spirals of smoke arising from different streets in Drumbron and knew my pals were having great *spraoi*. I opened the top part of the window quietly. Jock was playing his accordion and I heard screeches and laughing and voices happy to be celebrating the longest day of the year. I wished I was big and could do what I wanted. When my eyelids started to fall down on my eyes, I went into my bed. Just before my eyes shut, I saw Will on the mantlepiece. I wondered if Liam was having *spraoi* with his pals at the bonfire in the Home.

A few nights after bonfire night we had Sports Day. In the two-legged race me and Evelyn were laughing and falling the whole time. We didn't win the race but Regina and Noeleen, who were paired in the race, didn't win either. We didn't see Loretta around and thought maybe she didn't come to school. My egg keeping falling off the spoon, so I didn't win that race, but I nearly won the sack-race, only Declan Ganley, a boy from our class, got to the finishing line just a second before me.

Daddy said not to worry I had nearly won. "Coming second is not bad."

"Nearly never made it," Mammy said spoiling the lovely feeling I had inside. Daddy held my hand and we started to walk around the field while Mammy folded up the sack and left it with the other sacks. She caught up to us.

"Look, there's the Currys with their daughter, let's go and say hello," Mammy said, so we stopped and spoke to them. My mother called Evelyn's mother Margaret and Daddy knew Garda Curry from the barracks.

While they were talking, me and Evelyn ran to where Úna and Kait were jumping around.

"Are ye going up Clonthu Hill tomorrow?" I wanted to know.

"I can't cos we're going to the bog on the ass and cart," Úna said.

"Do ye have a cart?" I asked.

"We don't. Daddy got a loan of it from my uncle Mick."

"What do you do in the bog?"

"We help Daddy and Mick foot the turf and make reeks."

"Reeks like in Nan's house?"

"No, silly goose, small pileens of sods standing up against each other on the ground."

"What for?"

"To dry."

"Where do the sods come from?"

"Daddy cuts them out of the bog with a *sleán*, silly goose."

"I'm not a silly goose, only my daddy doesn't go to the bog, so I don't know."

"How do you get yer turf?"

"In a lorry from Mr Delaney."

"We buy bags of turf when Daddy comes back from Scotland with money, so we do," Kait said to show Úna not everyone went to the bog.

"Is it nice in the bog?"

"It is when we eat the hard-boiled eggs and drink the tea from the bottle but when the midgets are around, you get fed up scratching."

That evening at teatime Mammy said, "Margaret Curry is a lovely woman. I was telling her to send Evelyn here to play with you."

Sometimes my Mammy was smashing. I asked her, "Mammy, will I make a house in the back garden, so I can play in it with Evelyn?"

"That's a great idea. It'll keep ye entertained in the summer with no school to go to."

"Will you give me the old frying pan you're throwing out and I'll make dinner in it for me and Evelyn?"

"I will indeed. When I was small, we had a *tigín agus rudí go leor iar cul an tig*, eh, I mean a house and things in it."

Summertime was smashing. It was different because the weather was warm and there was plenty of time to do things, like going for walks, fishing in the river, dancing and singing, going to beach, visiting relatives and playing games.

The first few days of the holidays we played Tick, Hopscotch, Skipping and 'Queenio, Who's Got the Ballio' while Úna was in the bog. When all the turf was brought home, it meant we could play 'Ring A Ring A Roses' with Brendan and Teresa because we needed piles of children to make a big ring. Evelyn didn't know how to play *Buille*, so we showed her what to do.

"Evelyn, this is the *bata beag*, with the two ends sharpened like a pencil," I told her holding the small fat stick with the pointy ends on the palm of my hand.

"With the *bata fada* you *buille* the *bata beag* when it's coming at you through the air. When you miss and it falls to the ground, you need to bend down and hit one of the ends with the *bata fada* and make it jump up in the air."

"Evelyn, stand here on this half circle," I pointed to the half circle and the square box I had drawn on the path where we were playing.

"Alright."

"Now fling the *bata beag* to her."

Kait was standing in front of the square box, a bit away from Evelyn, holding the *bata fada* ready to *buille*. The *bata beag* fell beside Kait. She was never able to hit the small stick when it was in the air. Úna could sometimes, even though she wore glasses, so Kait used the long stick to hit one of the ends of the *bata beag*. It jumped up and Kait hit it again and it went flying through the air. While it was in the air, Kait tried to *buille* it again to make it go further away but she missed, and it fell on the ground.

"How many steps are you going to take to get to the *bata beag*?" Kait asked Evelyn.

"Seven."

"Come up to the square and start jumping from here."

Evelyn reached the *bata beag* in five because she took big steps. Then it was her turn to be *Buille*.

"This game is great *spraoi*, will we play it again tomorrow?" Evelyn asked us as we were getting ready to go home.

"Tomorrow, I'm going to the shops in Sligo with my Mammy and I can't play with ye," I told them.

When Mammy wanted to buy clothes, she went to the shops in Sligo with Mr Delaney in his car. At Mass and downtown, all my pals' mothers and everyone looked at Mammy's lovely clothes, but she didn't think she had enough dresses because she was always complaining to Daddy she had nothing to wear.

"The wardrobe is full of clothes, Dervla."

"It might be, but there isn't one decent thing in it."

"That suit you had for Arlene's communion is grand."

"William, if you think I'll be wearing it when I go to the Royal Hotel with Margaret Curry, you have another thing coming." Daddy didn't get a chance to answer because Mammy continued. "For your information, I haven't a notion of letting her think it's the only decent thing I have, so I'll be off to Sligo as soon as John is free.

"Ach…"

"And William, when we go to Cavan, I'll have no Protestant relations of yours looking down their nose at me because of the way I'm dressed."

"You know I can have the squad car anytime I like, and I'll take you shopping."

"Sure, wouldn't I be the right eejit sitting in the squad car looking like you arrested me."

"Dervla, look, I have to go to the barracks. We'll talk when I get home."

"If you see Gerry Curry ask him about the car he's buying."

"What car?"

"Margaret told me they are getting a car. It will be great altogether when an ordinary Garda has a car, and the sergeant doesn't."

On Saturday, Mammy was holding my hand and we were going to cross over to the Town Hall to put a penny in Jock's bag, when the beeping of a horn sounded behind us. We turned around and saw Daddy sitting in a square car, the belly nearly on the floor like Úna's pram, but in a straight line across and not round. The face of the car had a puss on it like a pug dog.

We rushed over. Daddy leaned across and opened the door on the other side of him. Then he pushed down the top part of the seat and told me to go into the back. Mammy sat in the front next to Daddy.

"Dervla, what do you think of this nice Mini?"

"Oh William, you never said a word. I hadn't a clue you were buying a car."

"I wanted to surprise you."

"I'm over the moon. Where did you buy it?"

"In Smith's garage. Will it take us to Cavan, do you think?"

"Oh William, we could go to Rome like Aubrey Hepburn!"

Daddy laughed and said, "Dervla, I know I look like Peter O'Toole, but I uphold the law, so no stealing millions!" Mammy looked puzzled, so Daddy said quickly, "Will we go for a spin to Sligo?"

Cavan

"William, I have to get my hair set when I'm finished here."

"What's the occasion?"

"You didn't forget we are going to Cavan."

"Ach, we not leaving until the eleventh. Get it done on Monday, the day before we leave."

"William, I'll be busy all day Monday packing and getting things ready. You said we were leaving early on Tuesday morning."

"Aye, so Arlene can be with her cousin Sammy and see the bonfire."

"Is there a bonfire? Do we need to collect stuff for it?" I said all excited thinking Úna and the others could help me find stuff and we could push it in the pram.

Daddy put his hand back and patted me on the head as he said to Mammy, "I'll drive you home to leave the messages and then to the hairdresser."

"That's grand. The news will be all over Drumbron as soon as Peggy sees the car," Mammy said, and Daddy laughed.

After Mammy finished in the hairdresser's, she went to the drapery shop and bought material and a pattern for a shift dress. At home she cut out the two dresses, one with sleeves and a belt and the other without, so they would not be the same. That evening she didn't pluck the chicken that was hanging on the back of the scullery door, because she had her head bent over the sewing machine, sewing away. When Daddy came home, she sent him with the chicken to Mrs McLoughlin. When he came back, she told him to go to the butcher's to buy a pound of meat for roasting, because she was up to her eyes finishing the dresses.

When she tried on the first dress, pink with a frill at the bottom and the neck, Daddy said she looked beautiful. While she was tacking the blue one, Daddy got me ready for bed so she could finish it that night, before she went to bed. When we were upstairs, I asked Daddy about the bonfire.

"Arlene, it's the biggest bonfire you'll ever see. We make a big tower and set it alight."

"Like in Drumbron?"

"It's bigger, it can be seen for miles around."

"Does it start after tea like the one here?"

"No, the big fire doesn't start until midnight."

"When Cinderella had to be at home?"

"Aye, so her chariot didn't change back into a pumpkin?"

"But I'll be in bed asleep."

"You won't because the wains have their wee fire early on. Sammy, your cousin will be there to mind you."

"I don't know Sammy."

"You will soon and your Aunt Hazel as well."

"Is Hazel your sister, Daddy?"

"She is and wee Sammy's mother."

"Is his name Sammy Blake, Daddy?"

"It's Sammy Sloan, like his daddy."

"Oh, but I'll just call him Sammy. What else are we going to do in Cavan?"

"We'll go to see a parade."

"That's smashing, like the one on St Patricks Day?"

"Aye but with bands and drums and music."

"Mammy likes music."

"She does but the drums are big and make lots of noise, so we mightn't tell Mammy me and you are going to the parade."

"Cos she'd get a headache."

"She might. Remember what I told you about not telling Mammy certain things, so we don't upset her and made her sick?"

"I do."

"Well, this is the same. You and I will be going to a different town to see the parade and Mammy will stay in Cavan with Aunt Hazel."

"Alright, Daddy."

"That's my wee lass, the best in all Ireland, England and broad Scotland."

The next morning Daddy drove us to Mass in his new car because Mammy had said, "William, as you are working today, wouldn't it be a good idea to drive up to the chapel and leave us as the door before you go to the barracks."

We passed Mrs Curry and Evelyn as they were entering the chapel grounds, so Mammy decided to wait at the door. The four of us went in together and walked up the middle aisle to the front rows. After Mass, me and Evelyn skipped and ran around while Mammy told Mrs Curry how busy she was preparing for the trip to Cavan in the new car. She had to pack all my nicest dresses and cardigan, as well as her own and Daddy's.

It was still dark outside when Mammy woke me up. I was too sleepy to eat breakfast and slept all the way, so I don't remember anything about the journey to Cavan.

When I opened my eyes, we were driving up a long lane with a house at the end of it. The house was as big as the Fitzgerald's Mansion in Drumbron and Daddy said his sister lived in it.

A big man called Simon, shook Daddy's hand and clapped him on the back. Daddy said he was my uncle because he was married to Hazel, his sister. Daddy held Mammy's hand and presented her to Simon. My uncle was tall and sandy-haired like Daddy. He was looking down on Mammy because she was small. He shook her hand and said, "She is as beautiful as you said, Will." and then turned to me, "So, this is your wee lassie, Will? She's a tall one, taking after the Blakes."

"Yes, she is tall, but her colouring is pure Galway," Mammy answered with a cross look.

My cousin Sammy was inside the house. He was small with blonde hair and light blue eyes like I had coloured Will, the little boy in the painting book.

My aunty Hazel bent down and said to me, "Arlene, you are going to share Sammy's room. I hope you don't mind."

"No Aunty, I'm happy I'm going to sleep in his room," I said and smiled at my cousin.

A woman came from another room and carried our suitcases upstairs. Sammy's room was enormous with carpet all over the floor like in the Royal Hotel. There were windows down to the floor. My bed was under one of the windows, real far away from Sammy's. Mammy went to the room she and Daddy were going to sleep in with the woman who she called Mrs Tuttle and their suitcase. I looked around surprised at how big the room was. Near the middle window, with no bed, a train set was spread out on the floor with tracks. There were toy trees and buildings and everything. It looked like a real town, only very small.

I told Sammy about the station in Drumbron and how me and my pals went up the tracks and played in the old graveyard. He kept asking about what we did. In the end, I changed his tracks around so it would it looked like the Drumbron Station. I used my fingers to walk along the tracks as though they were me and my pals. He wanted to be Úna because he said she sounded like the leader. We were lying on the floor walking on the tracks, our fingers jumping out of the way when a train came along, when there was a tapping at the door. Mrs Tuttle stood there and told us lunch was being served.

We went down for lunch, but it was really dinner. Afterwards me and Sammy ran out to the garden to play. The garden was as big as Castle Fields with plenty of trees. On the branch of one of the trees there was swing. I jumped up on it and told Sammy to push me. He wasn't very strong and only made me move back and forward a little bit. When I got tired of swinging on it, we played hide and seek among the trees. At the bottom of the trees a small stream ran over stones and pebbles. I told Sammy about our game of 'Who's the King of the Castle' and had great fun playing it.

After a good long while, the woman came to tell us dinner was ready. I sat between Mammy and Daddy at the same long table and we had supper, only they called it dinner. Mammy was smiling and talking to Aunt Hazel. The two of them liked Jackie Kennedy and were hoping Jack, her husband, would win the elections and become President of America.

Aunt Hazel laughed when she saw me eating, "I wish Samuel had as good an appetite as you do, Arlene."

"Arlene burns up everything she eats. She's always on the go." I looked at Mammy, it was the first time she ever called me Arlene, but she didn't seem to notice she changed my name. "William and I are delighted she is such a healthy child, although there are times she wears me out."

"You are fortunate. Samuel is poorly most of the time. We have discussed sending him to boarding school but the doctor believes we should wait a year."

"Aunt Hazel, Samuel is going to come to Drumbron because he wants to play with my friends."

"What a wonderful idea," Aunt Hazel said smiling but Mammy was looking at me as though she was trying to see inside my head.

After dinner, Mammy and Aunt Hazel went into the room that had a wall lined with books, from the ceiling to the floor. A lamp with glass, spidery legs hung from the ceiling and shone light on two beautiful pink armchairs, with wide backs, in front of a fire surrounded by a white mantlepiece. Aunt Hazel sat on one of the chairs and Mammy went to the other. Daddy brought me upstairs in case I wanted to do wee-wee. He got my cardigan out of the case and told me to put it on. When we went downstairs, I ran to Mammy and gave her a kiss. Aunt Hazel put her cheek out, so I kissed and hugged her as well. Then it was time to go the bonfire with Sammy.

The fire was up to the sky, a hundred times bigger than the ones Úna and Kait told me about. It was built with wooden boxes with wide slits in them like a garden gate. They were piled on top of each other, making a round tower, like the one that is outside Drumbron, in the place where the monks used to live. The flames leaped at the sides and there was a sound of crackling as the wooden pieces were blackened by the fire. The tablecloths of different colours hanging on the sides were burned into grey ashes, disappearing like pepper and salt among the red fire. It was smashing with sparks blowing about.

I took my cardigan off because the heat was making us all warm. When Daddy said it was time to go, I didn't want to leave. I fell asleep in the car and don't remember going to bed.

The next morning the woman, Mrs Tuttle, knocked on the door and came in to wake us. When the woman was dressing my cousin, Mammy came in to comb my hair and put on my communion shoes.

Then we had breakfast at the long table downstairs. Sammy didn't want to eat his sausages so I whispered to Aunt Hazel if I could have them. She looked at me with her eyes the same way Daddy looked at me and nodded her head. As I was wearing my communion shoes, I showed them to Aunt Hazel when I stood up and told her about my dress that Mammy had made. The car was parked outside the door and before I sat in the back seat with Sammy to go to the parade, I gave my auntie another hug.

In the town of the parade, I said to Daddy, "Look at all the tablecloths fluttering on the lamp posts." He laughed and said they were flags.

People filled the footpaths and were smiling and talking as they watched the bands banging drums and blowing tin whistles and marching along on the road. The parade was better than smashing. At the very beginning there was a big, huge banner with a gold fringe around it. It had a picture of a man dressed in a lovely, velvet jacket riding on a horse with its legs up in the air. The man looked beautiful with long, black, curly hair. The men who marched behind the banner wore suits and pot-round, black hats and some even had white gloves. They walked with umbrellas and had lovely orange ribbons on their chests and moved their legs stiffly but in time to the music. Plenty of the bands had only flutes and drums but a few had accordions. They were the best.

I whispered to Daddy, "I want to learn to play the accordion."

"You will, missy. I'll arrange for you to have classes with Pete Canny."

The parade was great fun like Sports Day at school. Everyone was happy and smiling even though the men playing the big drums, that nearly went down to the ground and up to their chins, had to be tired banging away real hard to make them sound like thunder.

"It's smashing here Daddy, why did we never come to Cavan before?"

"Ach, it's a long way to come for Mammy."

"But now we have a car."

"We do but before we didn't and besides, Mammy doesn't like Cavan."

"Why doesn't she?"

"She feels trapped between the hills."

"That's silly."

"People from the West are used to flat, open land. On our honeymoon, Mammy said she missed Galway."

"Did you fall in love with Mammy in Galway?"

"I did. The minute I set eyes on her."

"Did you meet her at a ball like the Prince met Cinderella?"

"You're a funny wee lass and before you ask, Mammy had no ugly sisters. Or brothers, just a mother and father."

"Did you go to the church in a chariot and have a wedding banquet like Cinderella and the Prince?"

"We got married at the side chapel in your mother's town."

"The part of the chapel where the confession boxes are and then you came to Cavan?" I said, thinking maybe that is why Mammy likes to go to the side chapel where the statue of Our Lady is.

"We did and Mrs Tuttle served us lunch when we arrived here for our honeymoon."

"Tell me about the wedding, Daddy?"

"When you are older I'll tell you, Arlene."

"I want to know now."

"Arlene, let's watch the parade."

I stamped my foot and put on the biggest puss I knew how to make but Daddy just kept looking at the parade and wouldn't tell me anything else about him and Mammy. I took the puss off because Daddy said, "Enjoy yourself now, because we have to leave Aunt Hazel's house this evening."

"I don't want to and besides Mammy doesn't have the case packed."

"She'll be ready when we go back."

We got home when it was dark. Daddy carried me into bed.

The next morning, I woke up because I heard the wheels of Úna's pram going up and down Suileen Road. I got up and dressed and went downstairs really quick. Mrs McLoughlin was in the kitchen and told me Mammy was still in bed because the journey had tired her out.

"Mrs McLoughlin, my pals are outside, and I want to talk to them for a minute."

"Do that, a girl, while I make you some toast."

I ran out the back gate and called them. Úna said we were going to celebrate I was back, by having a picnic under the bridge of the Suileen River.

"But we have no sandwiches or anything," I said.

"I do, so I do. Mammy gave me the heel of the loaf with jam on it and I have tea here," Kait said showing me a bottle with beige water and a newspaper stopper in the top of the neck. Úna had bread and jam too, so I told them to start walking while I got my toast and some biscuits from Mrs McLoughlin.

On the way to the river, they asked me if I got car sick on the way to Cavan. I said I didn't. Úna said she vomited when they went on the bus to see the eye-doctor. I told them about the parade and me and Kait started marching real stiff like the men in the round hats. Then Kait pushed the pram so Úna could march with me. When we got fed up with that we started climbing over the stone walls and running into the field and picking flowers and throwing ourselves on the grass and rolling about. Brendan and Teresa started getting cranky because they wanted to get out of the pram, so in the end we stopped playing and walked really quickly to get to the river.

As we got near, we saw a bunch of boys from St Jarlath's Avenue, on the bank. We waved to them and they waved back. The boys had their shoes off, so we took ours off too and waded into the water. The boys were fishing with lines and hooks and told us not to splash too much or we'd frighten the fish. Then they began acting real bossy, saying it was our fault the fish were not biting, so we put on our shoes and started to leave. As we were going, Seán, the bossiest one, said to Kait, "If ye come tomorrow, we'll show ye how to fish with a line and hook but ye need worms."

"I'm not bringing any dirty worms," Evelyn told him crossly.

"If you could get a small few for me, it would be great because I don't know where to find them," Kait said quietly and not cross at all like Evelyn was.

"A course I will," Seán told her, "I'll keep the good ones for you."

The next day we were there before the lads came. We saw them strolling along the road.

Úna wanted to know what kept them.

"We had to dig for the worms in the garden."

"Let me see them," Úna demanded. Seán held out a can of pinky-brown worms all wiggling and moving slowly.

"Where do we put them?" Evelyn asked, picking up a few of the worms and putting them onto her palm. The lads had four fat pieces of stick with a line wrapped around them.

"Here on the hook at the end of the gut," Kevin, another boy said, as he unwound the gut a small bit. There was a pointy hook tied onto the end of it.

"I can't do it, the worm is moving, and I don't want to touch it," Kait said in a small voice.

"No bother, I'll do for you," Seán said going over to her and picking out a worm from the can.

The other boys were good and put the worms on the hooks for us, except for Evelyn, who did it herself. We threw the line into the water. Seán helped Kait to throw hers in.

We sat on the bank waiting for the fish to bite. They weren't hungry, so we put the small, fat stick under a rock like the way Seán had showed us. We then skipped off to another field where there was a pond. The lads had jam jars and we scooped up tadpoles. After a while we went back to the lines but there weren't no fish on the hooks.

"Look at the *dearógs* swimming," Kevin said. There was a pile of baby fish swimming together. Seán put his hand in the water and said he was going to get some, but he couldn't. Kevin boasted, "We caught plenty of eels yesterday."

"Why didn't ye keep some to show us?" Úna wanted to know. We stayed half the day, but we didn't catch any eels, so we never got to see what they looked like. Kevin said they were grass-snakes that hid in the water when St Patrick banished all the serpents from Ireland.

"Where do you go to school, Kevin?" Evelyn wanted to know.

"The Brothers, me and Seán are in second class, next year we're going into third class."

"We're going into second next year, if we're not kept back."

"They don't keep anyone back in first class, but they do in second if you don't know how to read."

Kait got up from where we were sitting because she saw a tree in the middle in the other field and wanted to see if there was a fairy under it. Kevin and Seán jumped up and then Tom, who was leaning on a stone wall, moved and the three galloped over to the ditch she was trying to climb. They started to push each other because all of them wanted to help her.

Kait's leg touched a nettle and she cried out. Tom looked at her and went back to lean against the wall but the other two went looking for a dock leaf for her leg. They kept pushing each other to be the first to give it to Kait. After that they were half fighting again to spit on it and rub the burned part of her leg with it. When Kevin was rubbing Kait's leg with the dock leaf, he told her if she ever got cut and was bleeding, she had to put a cobweb on the cut to stop the bleeding. The rest of us got tired of looking at the lads making a *peata* out of Kait and we went back to where the jam jars with the tadpoles were.

"Lads, we are going to throw the tadpoles back into the pond, so they can grow up to be frogs," Evelyn shouted at them.

"A course." They didn't mind at all, and they helped us push the pram, so we got home quicker.

Kait Kenny's mammy had moved them to a house in Kilmartin Road because the crying from the Home Babies was driving her demented. Now Kait lived two streets away from me and only one away from Evelyn who lived in Sligo Road. It was smashing because Mrs Kenny let us play in her house.

One day me and Kait were playing house out Kait's back and Evelyn came running in to tell us the carnival was setting up in the green. That evening the four of us went. We walked around in the muddy field looking at all the swing-boats, go-cars, bumpers, ghost train and brightly coloured rides. Me and Evelyn had money, so we went on the swing boats and bumper cars but Úna and Kait had no money, so they looked and waved at us. After a while, they got fed up looking at us on the rides and went off because they heard music and singing coming from a stripy tent that had a peak in the middle and was tied to the ground with ropes.

They waited until we got off the swing boats and told us they were going to slope in under one of the side flaps to see who was singing. We went with them. It was dark inside, so we stayed hunched down, looking at the stage with lights at the far end. It was smashing. Girls with beautiful, frilly, lacy dresses came out on the stage and danced and sang. Then a man was falling and doing silly things. We laughed, clapped and shouted like all the people who were sitting on the benches.

After plenty of songs and dances, a man came on stage and thanked everyone for coming to the variety show and the girls and the men came out from the two sides of the stage and they sang 'There's no business like show business'.

On the way home Kait said she wanted to stage a variety show in her backyard.

"That's not fair, Kait. You know well I mind Brendan and Teresa every day and won't be able to be in it," Úna said.

"But Úna, they can play in our backyard while we are rehearsing, and they'll be quiet watching us."

From then we practiced singing 'There's no business like show business' and dancing, like we had seen them do in the concert on the square patch of cement floor outside Kait's backdoor. I showed my pals the Irish dancing steps from Miss Canny's School of Irish Dancing and Music, as well as two poems from the elocution class and we all knew the songs from The Walton's radio programme.

Thomas, Kait's big brother, hung a line across the front of the stage that was the square, cement patch. He hung a sheet on it as the curtain. Mrs Kenny said we could use the back-kitchen as the changing room. When we dressed up and came out the back door and sang and danced, Brendan and Teresa laughed and clapped their hands.

Úna and Evelyn said we were going to charge a button to everyone to see the show. Maura McLoughlin came with her brothers and sisters and put the buttons into the jam jar. Kait's cousins Shelia and Ciaran didn't have a button. We let them in free, because sometimes me and Kait went to their house on Kilmartin Road and their mammy, Eithne, gave us bread and jam. Seán, Kevin, Tom and the other lads from the river said they had no buttons, but they gave us a pile of worms, so we let them in.

They sat in front of the stage and started stamping their feet and whistling when Úna pulled the curtain and we appeared wearing long dresses and high heel shoes with lipstick on. She got trembly and whispered to us she was going back into the back-kitchen because the lads were mocking us but Kait said to wait and stepped out in front of us and in a shaky voice said, "Hey lads, we feel like right eejits and we are afraid we'll forget the words with the nerves, so don't be mocking us too much." Straight away she started singing 'There's no business like show business' and we joined in. When the lads learned it a bit, they joined in too. They clapped and cheered when we finished the song.

Kait was so happy she called down to them, "Come on up here and make the farting noises ye make with yer mouths."

The next day, everyone was talking about the show, so we did another one with the lads acting the eejit to make everyone laugh.

The summertime was smashing. I was out all day playing. Then one day Mr Delaney began his silly goose thing, saying, "We'll never feel until the days start getting short and the children are back at school." All because of him, Mammy told me to come in early from playing because she had to fit my dresses on and see if they needed letting down. The she bought me a new pair of shoes for going back to school.

"Mary, I'm glad school is starting next week because you are worn out with all the playing you are doing."

I was tired and sometimes when I went upstairs to bed, I fell asleep before I finished saying my prayers. I didn't remember to look at Will on the mantlepiece and because of that I sort of forgot about Liam until I went back to school and saw Brigid.

When we went back to school, all the boys were gone from our class to the Brothers, so I didn't see Liam. He would be up Cork Road in the Christian Brothers school with all the other boys because now we were big and in second class.

The first day at school, I had my new shoes on, and Evelyn had hers on too. They were the same kind as mine with lacers. Kait and Úna were still wearing their sandshoes. Everyone was looking at Loretta's shoes. They were shiny with a strap and a buckle. She was still small with the bouncy curly hair, so our new nun putting her sitting in the front row.

We were in second class with Sister Kevin. She was really skinny. Evelyn told us to be careful and not blow on her or she'd go flying like the leaves do in the wind. From the first day she made a *peata* of Úna, letting her give out the books and clean the blackboard. Maybe it was because the nun had thick glasses the same as Úna's ones. She wasn't a cross nun and was nice to everyone, even the girls on the bad side. She didn't look like she was going to vomit when she was beside the few girls from the Home that came back to school after the holidays.

Brigid was among the small group, but she was hidden inside herself, so it was no good looking at her, hoping she'd tell me something about Liam. If Brigid would come out of herself, I could talk to her because Sr Kevin was good and wouldn't mind. Some days the nun would give the Home-girls crusts and slices of bread with a smattering of jam before they went to their part of the yard.

"I bet the nun doesn't eat her own food. She keeps it for them," Evelyn said.

"Maybe."

"A course she does, that's why she's a bag of bones."

Liam was a bag of bones too. He was gone from our class to the Christian Brothers so I couldn't see him unless I went up the Cork Road and waited outside the school for the boys to come out.

I didn't want to because after school me and my pals were out playing. If it was raining drops as big as stones, we went into Kait's house until it stopped. Other times we rushed into her aunt Eithne's house. Only Eithne, Shelia and Ciaran lived in the house because their daddy slept in England. My daddy slept in our house because he worked in the barracks and came home in the evenings but some daddies on Kait's road, Kilmartin Road, and on Úna's road, Dun na Rí Road, slept in beds in England. They were only in their own houses for a while in summer and at Christmastime, but they sent letters every week.

Batt the postman brought Eithne a letter every Tuesday with thin, crispy sheets of paper full of writing and pounds notes stuffed in the middle of pages that came from Mr Ward. Around the times we were going to get holidays at Christmas or in the summer, Eithne would be happy and tell us, "Martin is coming home next week."

That was great news for us because Mr Ward always bought us an ice cream cone on the day he arrived, even if the wind was blowing or it was pelting out of the heavens. He must have known we used to let Shelia and Ciaran into our singsong and dance concert in Kait's backyard for free.

So, when we knew the day he was coming, we would hang around their house until we saw them heading to the station and trail behind and hang around with them on the platform until the train arrived. Mr Ward's head would be stuck out the train window long before it pulled into the station. While the noise of the brakes was filling the place, he'd jump off the train and in a leap was beside the children. Dropping his suitcase, he'd pick up Shelia and Ciaran and swing them around.

We'd try to the lift the case, but it wouldn't budge for us. He'd grab it when he put the children down and looked at Eithne. She would move closer to him and they would walk side by side as we left the station.

We followed them as they crossed over the road to Jimmy Moran's grocery shop, knowing we'd soon have an ice cream cone, with a chocolate flake stuck in the middle of the soft, sweet, swirly stuff. It was smashing to watch how the white, snowy cream twirled and swished out of the machine into the wafer cone held in Mr Moran's hand.

Eithne changed and became pretty while Martin was home. She wore dresses instead of the dark, blue overall, full of tiny flowers, that wrapped around her body. Mrs McLoughlin had the same type of apron that looked like it was a dress without sleeves when she was cleaning our kitchen or in her own house. Eithne must have hung it at the back of the wardrobe, like Daddy did with his Garda jacket, because we never saw her wearing it while Mr Ward was at home.

In summertime, they'd go to the bog together to bring home the turf, Kait Kenny's father had footed for them. Mr Ward and Eithne stacked it in a reek at the gable end of house.

"Now darling, at least you and the children will be warm during the winter months. Every time I put a shilling into the slot in the gas fire, I think of ye and know at least you're looking into a warm glow and not down on two bright bars."

It seems like Mr Ward was around for ages but then, all of sudden, we were walking down to the station behind him, with the suitcase dragging his arm down. Ciaran and Shelia would skip along but Eithne looked heavy like the case. The daddy and the mammy dumped themselves onto the wooden bench in the waiting room while we ran along the platform and into the toilets. The man who sold the tickets sat in a small box with a window with no glass and a counter. He tore off a ticket from a roll and passed it out onto the counter ledge and took the pounds and coins people gave him.

"It's coming, it's coming." We'd scream all excited as we leaned our upper bodies in the direction of where we heard the sound of the whistle.

"Be careful now and don't go too close the edge," Eithne would warn us but she and Mr Ward didn't budge from the wooden bench, until the hissing and long screeching that the wheels made grinding to a halt, told them to get up.

They came out slowly walking close to each other. Mr Ward held on to the bar at the side of the train door, holding his case in the other and went up the steps like an old man. He turned his head and looked at us all below him as he pulled his body up the steps and into the compartment. We'd rushed to the wide window as he opened the top part and put his face into the long, narrow space and looked at the mammy. She kept smiling up at him, telling him she was fine. When the train started to move, she ran along the platform until there was no more platform left.

In a snivelling voice, coming from deep in her throat, she'd tell Shelia and Ciaran to keep waving to Daddy. We jumped up and down and kept moving our hands above our heads until the train got small on the track. As we'd walk out the station, Eithne took the hankie out of her sleeve and squashed it up against her face.

Kait's daddy, Mr Kenny went away too, but we never went to the station to see him off because he was home again after a little while. It was always when we went into the new class with the new nun that he came back.

We knew when the leaves started fall, Kait would come to school with a new pair of boots instead of sandshoes, because her father was back from picking the praties in Scotland. He had money for her mammy and Kait got the new boots to wear for the cold weather.

Úna told us she'd get new boots when her mammy got the children's allowance. Úna's father didn't go to Scotland for money. He worked in his house with a last and a small hammer. People from the road came with their boots and shoes when they needed a new sole or heels put on. Mr McNulty could fix a broken arm too because he was the seventh son of a seventh son and he had the gift of setting bones.

Úna didn't get her new boots until we started going up the fields picking blackcurrants and red haws from the hawthorn bushes. The lads from the river, who lived in St Jarlath's Avenue near Kilmartin Road, went too and we played with them. It was smashing rolling down the ditches and jumping between the cow dungs Moola Connors' cows left all over the fields. On windy days, we ran with the wind pushing us and had races to see who got to the bottom of the field first. Before we went home, we'd go to where the blackberry bushes were growing on the ditches at the sides of the fields, and stuff ourselves full of berries. One day Kait scratched her hand with the thorns of the bushes. The boys told her they would gather the berries for her from then on and that way she wouldn't get scratched any more.

Storm Debbie

Maybe Debbie didn't like the bushes hurting Kait either, because a few days later she blew the bushes and trees down. People were talking about Debbie before she arrived. One day the man on the news said the big, windy woman Debbie might strike Ireland with strong gales but the next day the same man said she wouldn't come near us, as she was on her way to France. Mr Delaney was saying Debbie was strong enough to cut the power off to the houses and we would all be left without the light.

Daddy put candles in all the rooms with matches beside them and piles in the small room where Mammy was. She was sick again and sleeping downstairs. If the lights went out, Daddy said we would be in total darkness and he gave Mammy two torches and told her to keep them close by. Dr Kelly said gusts of wind of more than a hundred miles per hour were on their way and would uproot trees and blow sheds to pieces. This information made Mammy worried. She wanted Daddy to stay at home to mind us, but he couldn't. He and all the Garda had to be in barracks in case Debbie paid a visit to Ireland.

Even though people were hearing about Debbie causing damage in other countries, when she came, she wasn't bold, only a bit noisy at the beginning but then she got really mad. She screamed and howled and threw things around the place in Drumbron and the countryside. The day she went wild, I was home from school sitting in the kitchen.

First, I heard her wrap herself around the house trying to make it shake but it held onto the ground. Then she took her spite out on the spades and forks and shovels, lifting them up and dashing them against the walls in the backyard. She made the buckets and cans rattle and fly through the air. She strew tree branches and rubbish all over the place and blasted sods of turf out of the reek, even though Daddy had put rope across it to keep the turf down.

I ran into the bedroom to Mammy and we held on to each other as bold Debbie hit the house and pounded on the walls. Mammy trembled when the light quivered and went out. We were left in darkness and the radio shut up. In the silence inside the house, the sound of Debbie battering the house grew louder. I didn't hear the hens squawking, but Mammy must have because she cried out, "*Día ar sábhául*, the hen house!"

"What about it, Mammy?" I wondered why she was so worried about the hens that it had made her lapse back into Irish.

"The roof will be blown away."

"No Mammy, I heard Daddy telling Dr Kelly he had secured it down with ropes that had big heavy stones tied on to the bottom." While I was saying that we heard the almighty crash of a tree falling.

"*In ainm Dé!*" Mammy screamed.

"It's the tree across in the field," I said to calm her. The crash came from the other side of Suileen Lane where there were no houses.

The room was dark, making Mammy worse so I asked her for the torch. She had it under her pillow. Switching it on, I went over to the dressing table and got the big, red Christmas candle and lit it with the matches Daddy had placed beside it.

"Mammy, let's go to the kitchen. The range is in there."

"You're right, it will throw a glow and even if we run out of candles, we won't be in total darkness."

"Mammy, Daddy put candles and matches everywhere. There is a long, white one on the dresser, so let's go there and light it. It will last a long time and not burn down too soon."

Mammy got up slowly. The back of her nightdress was red. "Mary, go to the kitchen and I'll be there in a minute. I just want to put on some right clothes. If anyone came in and saw me in my nightdress, I'd die of shame."

"Sure Mammy, everyone is at home, afraid to go out in case they get blown away," I said as I lit two candles and left them on the mantlepiece, so she could see and then asked, "Where's Daddy?"

"In the barracks. With the storm causing havoc, all the Garda are needed," she said as she picked up some small towels from the box at the side of the bed.

After a bit she came into the kitchen walking shakily. We sat together at the table. I was colouring my book and

Mammy took out her rosary beads from the drawer. She started praying for all the people caught out in the storm. After a while, the whistle of the kettle as it started to sing on the range, made Mammy lift up her eyes.

"Mary, will you wet a drop of tea?"

"A course I will, Mammy, and I'll put some bread in case you're hungry."

She took two bites out of a slice and then said, "Hold me by the waist to help me walk back to the room, like a good girl." She walked very slowly. "Mary, you sleep here with me. It's better we are together." The wind was howling but we fell asleep.

The next morning Daddy called in to see how we were.

"Dervla, sure Galway looks like it was hit by bombs. In Tuam most of the buildings in the town are damaged. The storm was raging there for hours."

"William, when do you think we will have the light back on?"

"Hard to say. The ESB are working flat out."

"Did the storm reach Cavan?"

"It did, a tree fell on a woman in a car."

"The Lord save us from harm. Any word from Hazel?"

"Thank God, they safe and sound." After cleaning out the ashes, Daddy put more turf into the range and then said he had to leave. "The worst is over, Dervla. Now stay in bed, I'll get Mrs McLoughlin to call over and make you something to eat."

When we went back to school after the storm, all we did was talk about Debbie knocking down trees and throwing things all over the place. Úna said Debbie blew slates from the roof of the Home and at playtime we rushed over to the Home Babies in the yard to ask them. They didn't answer us. Evelyn said talking to them was like talking to the wall. Then she made us laugh by saying maybe a slate hit them on the head and knocked a screw out.

I told my pals about the tree in the field across from my house. In the evening, we went to see it. The roots were all up in the air, in a giant round circle of brown clay. It looked like a chocolate cake with creamy streaks going out from the centre and was big enough for Cuchulainn to eat.

After days of non-stop talking about Debbie, we forgot about her, like I was forgetting about Liam. I started forgetting about Liam when Mammy took away the colouring of Will, the little boy, from the mantlepiece. She told Mrs McLoughlin to put in the box where all my other pieces of art, as Daddy called the pictures I coloured, were. When I told him, we had drawing class two days a week in second class, he was delighted. One day Sr Kevin held my drawing up and said I had talent. When I went home, I told Daddy, "Sister Kevin said I have the makings of an artist in me."

"You have the making of a little devil in you, aye, that's what you have," he answered, tickling me.

Mammy said with a vexed face, "Putting silly notions into your head."

Sr Kevin put plenty of things into our heads. She taught us how to sound out a group of letters and put the sounds together to mean a word. One day I looked at the page and knew the letters in 'tomorrow' meant tomorrow without sounding it out. The same thing happened to my pals. One by one, we all began to know how to read.

Second class was smashing with no cats on mats or rats in hats but instead Sr Kevin told us stories from the Old Testament as good as the ones we saw at the matinees in the Odeon cinema on Sundays. The story about Joseph and his coat of many colours reminded me of Liam and his *geansaí* with the stripes of different coloured wool but the God in the Old Testament was always cross. He was like Sr Ignatius and chastising people. Jesus was nice. He helped people and made them walk again. He was like Sr Kevin.

Sr Kevin told us Ducking Night was really *Oíche Samhain*, a pagan custom, to celebrate the coming of the dark evenings. It was from the times before St Patrick came to Ireland and baptised us and made us Christians. Now it was changed to All Souls Day and was a Day of Obligation which meant it was like a Sunday and we had to go to Mass. Priests could say three Masses, she said as though that was very important, but the priests were always saying Masses. It was also a special day because people could pray and get indulgences for the souls in purgatory. You needed to say seven Hail Marys, seven Our Fathers and seven Glory Bes so a soul got an indulgence and got out of purgatory quicker. That was why the chapel stayed opened until late, and people went in and out of the church as often as they wanted and lit candles and prayed for their deceased relatives.

Mr Delaney and his mother knew plenty of souls in purgatory and spent all the evening going in and out of the chapel, getting indulgences for their friends and talking to people outside the chapel door who were going in and out too. None of my pals knew anyone in purgatory, so we weren't worried about getting them out.

Lighting candles was good fun. Me and Ev queued up behind the line of people and let our penny drop to make the clanky sound. Then we lit our candle with the wick of one that already had a flame. We waited until the top burned and got soft and the wax overflowed and started sliding down, making knots at the side of the candle, before we stuck it into the slot on the golden table, with all the other quivering lit ones. Úna and Kait had no money so they couldn't light a candle.

"We'll get some pennies when we go to the houses with the candles in the turnips, but by then it will be too late to get one of the indulgences," Úna said.

"It doesn't matter anyway cos we know no one in purgatory," Kait reasoned.

"We can go to the graveyard and pray for the dead, if ye want," I said so Kait and Úna wouldn't feel they weren't part of the All Souls Day.

"Sure, we were there yesterday, remember I won all the time we were playing 'I'm the king of the castle' on top of the graves?" Ev said, "And besides, we need to finish cutting out the faces in our turnips."

"Ya, and I have to look for something to disguise myself when we go out this evening in the dark," I said.

"Let's up go to Clonthu Hill instead of going to the graveyard," Kait said.

"I have to mind Brendan and Teresa, so I'll go home and get them and ye can go to the nannas houses afore me."

We got to the house really quick and Ev started drinking tea out of Nanny's tin mug. She reached her hand out for to take a piece of the barm breac but Kait told her, "Hey, greedy face, wait for Úna. Look, she's at the bottom of the hill and she might be the one to get the ring."

Úna appeared with her brother and sister. Her mammy was in hospital having another baby.

"Will they be home soon, *a rua*?" Nanny asked as she buttered the brack and gave a big, thick slice to each of us.

"Tomorrow, I think."

"*A cratur*, the fairies will be wanting the new baby. Say 'God bless him or her.' as quick as lighting if you hear someone praising the infant."

"What for?"

"The *daoine sibhe* takes babies and leave changelings in their place."

"What's a changeling?"

"An ugly creature the fairies don't want for themselves, *a stóir*, so remember my words and say, 'God bless him or her' every time."

At that moment Kait let a screech out of her. She had found the ring. "Nanny, this means I am the one getting married."

"It does, *a stóir*."

"Will you marry Seán or Kevin?" Úna asked.

"None of them. The boy I'm going to marry is Jim Smith."

"He doesn't go to the river. Why are you marrying him?" Ev said.

"Cos he's lovely."

"Boys are not lovely," Úna said.

"He is. He cured my leg when it got caught in the back wheel of Mary's bike." Kait's big sister, Mary, worked in Smith's house in the evening after school.

"One day Mammy was sick, and Mary had to take me to work with her after school because the doctor was in the room with Mammy all day."

"Did you go in the house with Mary?"

"No, I don't work in Smith's and I stayed outside in the street."

"Why didn't you go into the house?"

"In case Mrs Smith was cross with Mary."

"Mrs Fitzgerald gets cross with my cousin Lina," Úna said.

"The street where the Smiths live is not like our street and no one goes into other houses."

"It's where the big shots live."

"It is."

"Were you frightened out on the street?"

"A bit when it started getting a small bit dark."

"I would be too," Úna said.

"And then a bunch of boys came along and started calling me names."

"What did you do, Kait?"

"I told them to stop and that's when Richard Martin hit me."

"I hated the guts out of that fellow and the other one he's always with, Kevin Fitzgerald," I said. Kevin was Loretta's brother and that was what made me not like him.

"Ya I do too, but Jim Smith pushed him and said boys shouldn't hit girls."

"Was Jim Smith with the other lads?"

"Ya he was, but he told Richard he'd belt him if he hit me again."

"Why didn't you call Mary?"

"I didn't cos she was working. Anyway, she came out with the bike when she was finished and told me to sit on the seat and we'd go home."

"And only for that, you are going to marry him?" Úna asked surprised.

"No, he gave me his catapult when my leg got caught in the spokes."

"That time or another time?" Úna wanted to know.

"That time. I was crying and wiping my face with my sleeve cos of Richard Martin and I forgot to keep my legs out, so I did, and one got caught in the spokes."

"You twisted your leg. You could end up lame like Mick the Sticks," Ev said.

"No, I got better quick cos Jim Smith gave me his catapult."

"Who wants an old catapult?" Kait pretended she didn't hear me say that.

"Jim Smith told me my leg would be really sore for a little while, then it would be a small bit sore and then get better."

"Did it?"

"It did, really quick."

Nan said to Nanny, "Isn't it young she is to be falling in love?" Then she warned us about the woods near Cnocmaigh, where Queen Maeve lives. "*A leanaí*, be sure ye have salt in yer pockets when ye go gathering hazelnuts in that woods."

"What for?" I asked.

"It's a fairy wood and if the little rascals are up to devilment, they'll take yer souls."

"They will so they will. They took Mick the Sticks leg when he fell asleep under a tree," Kait told us.

"*A cailíní*, ye that are young and well able to move about, will ye light a candle for the soul of my Jack?" Nan said.

"A course we will. The chapel is opened until it gets well dark."

As we were leaving, Nan told us Nanny Ward found the stick in the barm breac.

"What does that mean?" Ev leaned close to Nan to hear what it meant.

"That she'll be making a journey."

"Devil the journey, I'll be making if it's not to the graveyard."

"The barm breac doesn't lie and you know that well."

We left the nannas talking and ran down to the chapel. It was full of people going in and out the opened doors. I prayed and lit a candle for Mammy to get better and go upstairs with Daddy. I told God he had to make her better, because I wouldn't be able to slope out and go with my pals if she was sleeping downstairs. She was sure to hear me opening the door, like the night of the storm when she heard the hens. The money on the candle was wasted because Mammy didn't get better. I wasn't able to go house to house with the turnip on Ducking Night.

A short while after Ducking Night, the Home Babies stopped coming to school. First, we thought they all had measles and were sick in bed, but they never came back. I asked Mammy if Mr Delaney knew what happened.

"He told me the Home got damaged during the storm and they had to close it."

"Was it uprooted like the tree on Suileen Lane?"

"Mary, have a bit of sense, of course it wasn't uprooted, it's because the roof is collapsing."

"Falling in?"

"That's right."

"Did the roof fall on top of the children and hurt them?" I said, thinking of the woman and the child, who the man on the news said were killed in Cavan during the storm.

"It didn't, thank God."

"And the babies, where are they gone?"

"You can be sure they are well cared for, and Mary, the less said about certain things the better."

"Why?"

"Curiosity killed the cat, Mary."

"But Mammy…"

"That's enough out of you."

Nan and Nanny were like Mr Delaney and knew everything that was happening in Drumbron and on top of that, they didn't mind talking. They told us what happened to the roof in The Home.

"Nan, did ya know the roof of The Home got broken during the storm and all the Home Babies are gone."

"Arrah musha, we might be getting old but if they think they're codding people saying it was the broken roof that closed The Home, we'll let them, *mar dhea*."

"What was it closed for?"

"A visit late one evening closed it."

"How did a visit close it, Nan?"

"The inspector took it into his head to pay a surprise visit and that is what got it shut down," Nanny said.

"And the two other men he dragged along with him, Mary."

"Was the inspector big like Cú Chulainn?"

"Why are you saying that, a girl?"

"The inspector dragged the two men, so he was big to be able to pull them along with him."

"*A grá mo croí*, it's a way of saying he got them to go against their will."

Nan saw we still didn't know what she meant. "He fooled the two men into going to The Home unbeknownst to the nuns."

"What did it matter if the nuns knew the men were coming or not coming?" I asked.

"They didn't have time to hide the sick craturs away like they did at the other times, when they knew the inspectors were coming."

"What sick craturs?"

"The little children that weren't right, even though they came into the world as healthy as you or me."

Nanny Ward gave Nan a look and said, "*Ná bé ag caint, tá na clasaí mór ar na páistí agus beal na more ar guid.*"

"Off with ye now and keep yer mouths closed about what ye hear me say."

"But where are the Home Babies now, Nanny?" I screamed and stamped my foot.

"Isn't it you that's got the temper. The children went to other Homes."

"There's no other Homes, only that one," Úna, who knew everything, said.

"There is in other towns."

"In other towns, are you sure?" Ev, who also knew everything, asked.

"I am. The nuns have Homes in different parts of the country."

"Does that mean they are coming back when the roof is fixed?" I asked because I didn't know anything.

"It doesn't. They won't be back, *a leanbh*."

Liam was gone for good, like my little brother was gone with the babies with no names. I remembered the day in the toilets and how I had stopped Loretta mocking him. I was small then in first class and I didn't know how to read or go to confession. Now I was big, in second class. I had a gang of friends and a cousin in Cavan but still no brother. Brigid had Liam for her brother. It wasn't fair. I was starting to put a puss on when Nan Gormley said as though she was seeing inside me, "Arlene, when we love someone, they are always in our hearts." Nan was right because even though I never saw Liam again, I think about him plenty of times.

Primary School 1969 – 1972

The years went by and we grew big, not knowing, nor caring, what life had in store for us. We threw ourselves into it each day with gusto and slept holding onto what had happened that day, our minds full of the adventures we had lived and dreaming of the ones to come. Our lives weren't signposted by years but carved into our minds by the events taking place around us. After the Big Storm, no body-pushing, tree-shaking, roof-raising, bins-scattering and shattering gusty winds could keep us inside looking out – like Hurricane Debbie had done. She, along with our First Holy Communion, was carved into our minds as one of the most remarkable signposts along our childhood.

Making our Confirmation was a pale imitation of our First Holy Communion. It lacked all the excitement and tingling anticipation of the happiest day of our lives. As we moved from class to class, we were taught by different nuns of different hues, but none ousted Sister Ignatius or Sister Kevin from our memories. We played with other children, even let them become part of our gang, but we never shared our hearts with them. Evelyn, Kait, Úna and I remained the best of friends while people and things around us were changing.

We went into third class. Our nun's name was Sr Rita. She had a man's face, but she didn't get cross with anyone. Loretta and her pals were her favourites. They sat in the front desk, so the nun could smile at them and look at their lessons to see if they were right. Loretta knew 3x2 was six, but never learned that 3x3 was nine.

Sr Rita always asks her, "What is 3x2, Loretta?"

"Six, Sister."

One time, Sr Rita asked her, "2x3, Loretta?" She said she didn't know and when the nun prompted her, saying she did know, she answered, "Seven, Sister."

Then one day, when I was in the middle of third class, Daddy stopped wearing his uniform. He hung the dark-blue jacket with the brass buttons at the back of the wardrobe and it disappeared from our lives. In the mornings, he came downstairs dressed in a suit, looking like a film star. The first morning I couldn't stop staring at him. He put his hand on my head and ruffled my hair saying, "I'm still Daddy, pet, clothes don't maketh man."

When he was leaving for work, I followed him into the hall and watched as he picked up his hat and put it on his head. Daddy placed his first finger in the dent in the middle and the rest of them at one side. His thumb went on the other side. I called it his hilly cap, but he told me it was a trilby hat. As well as swapping his blue peaked cap for the hat, he used the car to go to work. The bike was in the hen house where the chickens used to be. The shed was empty. The hens were gone away like the Home Babies.

Even though Daddy changed his uniform for a suit, he didn't change himself. In the evenings he still went playing cards in the parish hall and to train the under-16 GAA players. I wanted to go with him to the pitch. He told me it was better I didn't because some nights he was out until bedtime. If I wasn't at home until that late time of night, Mammy might worry. She had been very *brónach*, which Dr Kelly called depressed since President Kennedy's assassination was shown on television. He was shot in Dallas, and Mammy kept talking about Jackie and how her lovely pink suit got ruined. Daddy didn't give a sugar about the Kennedys. He had told me the Kennedy's father was a criminal whose fortune came from bootlegging, which meant selling drink. He had no time for Rose Kennedy either, saying she was very ambitious for her sons but didn't care one bit if her daughter was locked up. Mammy loved the Kennedys, though.

Before Christmas, when the news of President Kennedy's assassination was shown on television, the *brónach* came on Mammy then and she didn't want to get up from bed. She lost her appetite. When she didn't want to watch Gay Byrne on television, Daddy and Mrs McLoughlin became worried. After much talk, serious looks from Daddy and nodding from the housekeeper, they decided to make up the room downstairs so Mammy would not be on her own upstairs. She could listen to the radio and to Mrs McLoughlin rattling about in the kitchen and see Batt when he came with the post.

For a good while, Mammy spent the whole time in the downstairs bedroom, looking at photos of the American President, Jackie, Caroline and John-John and wondering how they were coping. The photos of Jackie's pink Chanel suit, covered in blood, caused her to burst out crying. Daddy didn't know what to say to make her stop sobbing. She only got up when Mr Delaney called in to see her. Him and Terry Wogan on the radio, were the only people she wanted to listen to. And it was thanks to Mr Delaney she started to stop crying. He assured her that the White House staff had put bread soda and water on the dark spots on Jackie's suit, saying it was the best for removing blood stains, even though he had heard his mother mention that red wine could do the trick too. She looked at him and said, "Oh John!" Daddy looked at the two of them, shook his head and headed for the door. When Daddy came home late at night, he crept upstairs to their room next to mine while she was asleep downstairs.

Mammy became less *brónach* with Mr Delaney's visits and the magazines, full of pictures of the Kennedy family, that he brought her when he called to see her every evening. However, the day he bought the ones with Jackie, Caroline and John-John at the funeral was a bad day for Mammy. She said she would never wear pink again, but Mr Delaney warned her against doing such a thing.

"Dervla, you know pink is one of the best colours for dark-haired women. Assumpta Burke, you know the brunette woman, always wears pink and she is considered a real beauty."

"Is that at Mass, John, she wears it?"

"At the golf-club, never misses a day. My mother is very fond of her."

"I didn't know you played golf, John."

"I go there with my mother. I'd say you would make a great golfer, Dervla."

"Why do you think that, John?"

"You've got the arms to swing a club, if anyone has them."

They started talking about the golf course and the wonderful people who were members.

"Dervla, why don't you come along with me and you'll see for yourself what a fantastic crowd of people go there? The Annual Christmas Dinner Dance is on this Friday."

"John, I couldn't possibly go dancing so soon after Jack's death. I don't want to set people's tongues wagging."

"You are absolutely right, it would be very thoughtless of you."

"I wish William was as understanding as you, John. He doesn't know how difficult it is for me since Jack's death."

"Mrs Fitzgerald feels the same way as you do, Dervla."

Mammy lifted her eyelids and looked at him with interest. "Why don't you come along with me one of these days and have a chat with her and at the same you can try the coffee and give me your opinion on it."

The evening of her first day at the club, she came home looking beautiful with shining eyes and a smile on her face, and told Daddy, "William, I felt so proud when John introduced me to the other members as Mrs Dervla Blake, the Superintendent's wife. Mrs Fitzgerald was there, and she actually walked over to where I was standing and welcomed me to the club."

After that, she was the club every day chatting to other women. Now she had a gang of pals that she went with. The golf course was a bit outside of town, so Mr Delaney drove Mammy to it. A while after Christmas she said to Daddy, "William, Mrs Fitzgerald drives herself in and out of town, so I was thinking you could teach me to drive the Mini." Daddy agreed, but never found the time, so in the end it was Mr Delaney who taught my mother. Around town he was known to drive as slow and carefully as the hearse. His slow-motion pace might have been the reason Mammy was driving by summertime. During the holidays, she spent all her time at the golf club, and I played with my pals. We made picnics, went to the river, to the dump and to the sandhills near Barna Dearg where there was an old broken-down castle, as well as going up Clonthu Hill to see the nannas.

Mammy faded from my life like the warm, yellow brightness you see every morning in summertime that quietly turns into grey days and black evenings of the cold weather. She used to be standing in the light I woke up to. Her back bent over the Singer sewing machine greeted me when I rushed in the door from school. Her voice gave out to me for a hundred different things I did wrong. She made sure I said my prayers before I went to sleep. After she started playing golf, there was less of her about the house, like a candle in front of a statue that burns smaller and smaller.

Daddy coming into my room and touching me on the shoulder, telling me it was time to get up for school was the start of Mammy not being around so much. Some mornings I would see her in the kitchen in her nightdress and housecoat making toast. Those days she saw me off to school, but it was always to Mrs McLoughlin's house that I went to for dinner, that Mammy now called lunch, because she was in the golf course, lunching with her pals.

After school in the evening, it was Mrs McLoughlin's voice I heard saying, "Mary, a girl, the door can be opened without you taking it off the hinges!" when I pushed the front door in. It was the housekeeper who picked up my school bag after I flung it on the stairs, in the hall, as I rushed into the kitchen to grab something to eat.

"You know it wouldn't kill you to sit down at the table to eat that. You are like a dog with a bone!" she called after me as I galloped out the door carrying the ham and cheese sandwich she had made. "Where are you off to in such a hurry?" she'd ask knowing full well I was going to see Kait, Úna and Evelyn. At the beginning when I came home from school, Mrs McLoughlin would try to get me to do my lessons, but I explained to her that I didn't need to do any.

"Are you sure you're not making that up?"

"A course I'm not, Mrs McLoughlin. If there's a knock on the classroom door, Sister Rita nods to me, meaning she wants me to continue telling the class what she was reading from her book and then she goes outside to speak to the person at the door."

"Well, that's hard to believe but you always get good marks so there might be truth in it," she said smiling so I knew she believed me.

"With Sr Kevin in second class, we did the stories from The Old Testament. I knew the Seven Plagues and about Moses and how Abraham was going to kill his son to please God. And I know about Art O'Neill and Red Hugh O'Donnell escaping from Dublin and getting frozen in the hills and the Statue of Kilkenny."

"A pity you don't learn how to put your schoolbag in the right place."

"I will tomorrow, I promise."

"You'd better or I might have a word with that cross God of the Old Testament about you throwing your schoolbag on the stairs." But she was only codding because she was laughing and saying, "He knew how to punish people when they broke a rule."

There were rules everywhere and Mammy had to learn the rules of a card game called Bridge. She played it with her gang of friends in the evening and that meant I was with Mrs McLoughlin. The housekeeper taught me how to prepare myself for bed and to get my clothes ready for the next day. At night, I never forgot to say my prayers even if

Mammy wasn't sitting at the side of the bed. I was positive she gave me a kiss when she came home, only her lips were so soft they didn't wake me.

Mammy was still sleeping downstairs the night I had a bad dream about Liam. His eyes, big and wide, were staring at me. He was begging me to do something for him.

"Liam, stop looking at me and tell me what you want?" I screamed when I could get my voice out. Daddy heard me and came to sooth me. I pushed him away, murmuring, "Where's Mammy? I want Mammy."

"Hush, Arlene, when Mammy comes home, she is always tired. Climbing the stairs is too much for her. We had a little chat and decided it's better she sleeps downstairs."

"You're strong, Daddy, you could carry her up the stairs."

"Aye, lassie I could, but what about the nights when I'm out working in the barracks. I don't come home until the wee hours."

"She could sleep on the sofa until you come home."

"It wouldn't be good for Mammy to be waking her up."

"You mean she might get sick, Daddy?" I asked and when I saw him nodding his head, I knew he didn't want her to get sick.

Mammy was getting better and she stopped going off to hospital in the ambulance and Mrs McLoughlin stopped coming to our house in the evenings. She didn't want Maura and Catherine to be on their own, so she started washing and ironing our clothes in her house. And that is why after school, I went to their house until the evening-time when Daddy came for me and I went home to sleep.

Nothing was like it used to be, everything had changed, even our house. The shed was empty with only Daddy's bike put in there to get it out of the way. At least it wouldn't get dirty cos there was no chickens to poop on it on account of Mammy not buying the baby-chicks that came in a box on the bus from Dublin. She didn't pluck them and burn the feathers in the fire. The chicken we had for Sunday dinner came from a big, big shop called a supermarket.

We stopped going to the market on *An Lár* when the supermarket opened up near the Castle Fields. There was everything in it, even baldy chickens with no feathers. It was a big, big grocery shop with narrow hallways with walls of shelves. They were packed with tins and bottles and packets and toilet paper. People picked up a basket on the way in and walked along the aisle taking what they wanted from the shelves at the sides. The meat and naked chickens weren't on the shelves but behind a glass counter. A butcher with a cap weighed them and gave them to the mammies. Mammy drove to the new shop and on Sundays she drove to Mass. After Mass, we still had roast chicken with peas and jelly and custard for dessert because on Sunday Mammy stayed at home and cooked our dinner.

Mammy shrunk while Mrs McLoughlin stretched around my life. She became like Kait's and Úna's mammies for me. We shared looks that only we knew what they meant, like without ever saying in words that she had no *meas* on Mr Delaney. When she started sweeping around the chair he was sitting on and making him lift his feet or banging hard against the back of it with her brush, she was doing it on purpose, and I knew it. Her habit of forgetting to bring him his cup of tea until it was cold or telling him there was only enough Chester cake left for Mr Blake, was to spite him, as well as putting the radio on real loud when Mr Delaney was saying he had his 'own thinking' about the wedding that took place during Lent or that he knew the real reason why such and such a girl was going to England to their aunts' houses. I didn't have an aunt in England to go to when the men came into our house to build the extension Mammy wanted, so Daddy sent me to the McLoughlin's. One morning the men appeared, and the house became full of noise and dust as they started banging away making the new bedroom and bathroom. Daddy told Mammy I was in the men's way and I'd be better off with the McLoughlin's.

We got the new part added on because Mammy's gang of friends, from the golf club, couldn't go to the toilet in our house.

"William, I go to my friends' houses for elevenses, but how in God's name can I invite them here for coffee?"

"Why can't you? This is a fine house," he said from behind his newspaper.

"Fine! I'd be ashamed to invite any of them to this place."

"Ashamed?" He lowered the paper and looked at her with a serious face.

"Yes, ashamed. If they asked me to use the bathroom, I'd look a right eejit saying we don't have one."

"Don't we have a toilet? Surely to God they are not coming here for a bath!"

Mammy started sniffing and took out her hankie. Daddy ducked behind his paper and didn't say anything else.

"William, why do you speak to me like that?" Mammy said in a half crying voice.

"Sorry." The paper went down for a minute.

Mammy said, "I only wish you saw the bathroom they have in the Burke's and you'd understand why it would be lovely to have one too."

"The Burke's?" Daddy asked surprised, lowering the paper again. Mr Burke was the manager of the bank that went around the corner on Barrack Street and Cork Road.

"I was at a coffee morning in Assumpta Burke's house yesterday. I couldn't get over the lovely bathroom they have."

"Good for them."

Mammy pretended she didn't hear him. "Assumpta told me Joe Daly did the work and it didn't cost as much as she thought it would."

From then on, every chance Mammy got, she told Daddy how Joe Daly did this thing and that thing in her friends' houses, until one morning Daddy said, "Joe Daly wouldn't be available for a good few months, Dervla, so when we build the extension, I'll get Gerry Curry to do the job."

"Why's that, William? I hope Joe is not sick?"

"No, nothing like that. The nuns have him contracted to knock down the thick wall which hides the nuns residence from view."

"Is it the wall with the spikes of glass on top, Daddy?" I asked.

"The very one, Arlene."

"Why are they getting rid of it. Mr Delaney said the high, thick, glass-crowned wall is to keep the nuns safe, Daddy?"

"Safe from whom? Thank God that Pope of yers, John XXIII, has a bit of sense."

Mammy frowned but Daddy didn't see her, *mar dhea*.

"About time the nuns were let live like normal people and not having them locked up behind walls," said Daddy.

I saw Mammy's face tighten and I knew she was going to give out to Daddy, so I said really quick, "But our school is nice and normal, isn't it, Mammy?"

My primary school, with the gate going out to Cork Road, had a low white wall and railings around it. It did not have a high wall around it like the old school and the nuns' residence did.

"Of course it is, Mary, and you are lucky to have the nuns teaching you. So William, you want Gerry Curry to build the extension?"

"If you agree, we'll get Gerry to do the work. It's better the money goes into his pocket than to anyone else's."

"Whatever you want, William. I must tell Margaret when I see her today."

Garda Curry, Evelyn's daddy, came when he wasn't on duty with another Garda and built the extension. While Mr Curry was wallpapering the walls and painting the doors and windows and putting in new floors, Mammy and Mr Delaney were buying new carpets, curtains, lamps and piles of things Daddy said we didn't need.

Garda Curry was changing our house and making the old part nice and new-looking and Joe Daly and the men were changing the convent. They knocked down the high wall of big, thick stones around the house where the nuns lived, near the chapel. It reached up past everyone's heads to the sky. When it was gone, they built a low, pebble-dashed white wall with railings like the one in the primary school. The solid, black gate on the chapel side was changed for two wide ones with a design that looked like metal cobwebs. Now there was only one high wall with pointy, broken glass bottles on top of it in Church Street, on the path in front of Wynn's Bakery and Cafe.

The first Sunday after the wall disappeared, the people going to Mass couldn't believe their eyes when they saw the nun's residence across from the chapel. It looked like a mansion, the same as the Fitzgerald's house, with a tarmac driveway, wide enough to let the priest's car drive on it and park in front of the door of the nuns' residence.

Mr Delaney and Mammy didn't like the new wall, saying the light and sights of the outside world would pass through to the nuns and corrupt them. According to them, it would be more in the Pope's line to leave things the way they were. Everyone liked the Pope except them. He looked a bit like Úna's baby in the pram with a fat belly on him and always smiling and thinking how to make the Mass better. He didn't mind if women didn't wear scarfs on their heads and he let the nuns wear normal skirts.

At the beginning of summer when we were nearly finished third class, Pope John XXIII died. It was strange he died because it is only old people who die. Úna said he might not be dead at all, but he was, because during the summer, the big people kept crying and lamenting that it was always the good that were taken. Kait was holy and knew holy things, so when she said, "The Pope died on us." we were thinking he might be really dead. To make things worse, the first day we were back in fourth class, Sr Leo said a prayer for the dead Pope.

"Kait, why do we have to pray for him if he is already in heaven?" I asked her because she knew holy things. "Sr Kevin and Sr Rita only told us to pray for the souls in purgatory and for sinners."

"We pray to him cos he is our friend, and he will help us if we ask him."

Kait knew about saints and prayers, so I believed her. We missed Pope John XXIII and a *brónach* came on us, a heaviness that made us drag our feet. We didn't push each other or burst out laughing and lost all the lightness and the happiness that was inside us. It was nearly like as if the fairies had taken away our souls. Mr Delaney wasn't sad, and Mammy just said, "I hope Pope Paul will put things back the way they were." She said that because she blamed the Second Vatican Council for everything she didn't like.

"Women wouldn't be going around looking like men with trousers on them if it wasn't for that John XXIII and his Vatican Council," Mr Delaney said.

"And the young lads going blind with the hair falling into their eyes."

"Talking about hair, did you see how the girls going to Mass wearing a mantilla instead of a scarf or hat and the mean skirts that leave their knees showing, Dervla."

"Miniskirts, John. That's what they call them."

"Makes sense alright to call them skirteens mini."

"I can't, for the life of me, understand the carry-on of the young girls, pulling their hair out and jumping up and down when they listen to the awful music."

"It's them hooligans from Liverpool singing 'Love, love me do.' that makes them demented, screaming worse than the inmates in Ballinacora."

"That Vatican Council has a lot to answer for, John."

"Indeed, it does, with all the changes it's bringing in."

Mammy didn't like the changes in the church, but she liked the changes in our house. Once the extension was finished and the new furniture in place, our house looked completely different. Mammy started inviting her friends in for elevenses, serving them Italian coffee made in the percolator Mr Delaney had brough her back from Rome.

Mr Delaney and his mother were the only people in Drumbron who had been to Rome. They were treated like the holy relics, the tiny pieces of gauze cloth that had touched a saint's bone, because their eyes had rested on His Holiness, God's representative on earth. People stopped Mr Delaney in the street looking at him as though he had returned from heaven. He told them how the square, in front of the Papal Palace had been thronged with people looking at the Pope framed in the window. His Holiness lifted his eyes and gazed directly at Mr Delaney and his mother, lifted his hand, made the sign of the cross and blessed them.

Mammy's gang of friends were delighted to hear Mr Delaney talking about his visit to the Pope, but what impressed them more was him going into raptures about the exquisite coffee he made in the Italian coffeemaker he had brought from Rome. The black coffee-pot looked like the body of a fat woman with a small waist, wearing a skirt like the nannas wore. She had no neck and a tiny knob of a head on her broad shoulders. Mammy's friends would watch as Mr Delaney spooned shiny, brown beans into a metal box, placed its lid on and started to turn and twist around the handle on the top of the grinder. The kitchen would be filled with a wonderful aroma of the ground coffee beans.

Mr Delaney would pick up the coffee pot and, with a great flourish, unscrewed the bottom, skirt part of it. Then like a showman, he would turn the bottom upside down and shake out a flattish-cup thing with a tube in the middle. Holding the skirt part, for Mammy's friend to see, he would go to the sink, turn the tap on and fill it with cold water. Back at the worktop he would spoon the ground coffee into the round, middle, cup part, replace it back into the skirt part, and then screw the top part, with the handle and lid, back onto the bottom skirt part before placing the pot on the burner.

The first few times Mr Delaney demonstrated his technique, me and Evelyn were among the audience in the kitchen. We watched in awe as the coffee pot was put on the cooker and waited for it to boil. The percolator didn't sing like a kettle when it was boiling but bubbled and made gurgling sounds. In the steam that came from the triangular snout on the lid, there was a woody smell. Mr Delaney walked around the kitchen moving his fingers in front of his nose saying the delicious aroma, filling the kitchen, reminded him of the lovely, little, outdoor cafes that lined the street in Rome.

One day in the yard, me and Evelyn were telling Kait and Úna about the coffee and the going-on of Mr Delaney. Kait laughed and said, "If he had to smell my brother's farts in the bed, he'd be running from the house with his hand in front of his nose."

"And from mine too," Úna said. "Next summer my cousins are coming from Liverpool for the holidays, so we'll all be stuck in the same bed with no room to move."

"My uncle Martin is coming too but he stays in his own house," Kait said. Her uncle Martin Ward had his house in Drumbron but slept in England nearly all the time, cos he worked there and was only home in the summer and at Christmastime.

The summer came when third class finished, and Mr Ward arrived home on the train as usual. We all crowded into Moran's shop for our ice-cream cones. Kait's uncle said, "You wouldn't have any cardboards boxes you wouldn't be needing, would you now, Jimmy?"

"I do, Martin, I do. I'm getting a lot of people asking me for them lately."

"Sure, with the way things are I'm not surprised."

"I won't ask you what you want the boxes for."

"It's no secret. I want to pack a few things from the house in boxes and crates."

"You're another one thinking of leaving us for good."

"I am."

"Hey, ye young ones, when ye're finished the ice-creams, go out the back and get the boxes I have stacked up in the wool warehouse."

"Daddy, I want to go with you to see what you have for me in the suitcase," Shelia said to her father.

"No fear of ye not coming home with Mammy and me, Shelia, my little one. Kait, will ya be a good girl and get the boxes while we head on home?"

"A course we will," we said galloping out the shop and around the back to the courtyard where there was a stone building full of square, cloth bundles packed tight with wool.

"Let's sit on that bale there to eat our ice creams," Úna said as bossy as always. We ran and sat down on one of the smaller ones she was pointing to that was thrown on the stone floor.

"Úna, you're right."

"A course I am. Shur, we'll need our hands free to carry the boxes," she said as she held up her cone and started licking the sides. The melting ice-cream was dripping down the outside of the wafer cone. Me, Kait and Ev started doing the same to our own ones and had no time to talk we were so busy.

Voices, coming from on top of our heads, shouted, "Ah go on, give us a lick."

We looked up. Two faces were staring down on us. They had no bodies, like the angels in the crib at Christmas time with no bodies only wings under their fat heads. Mammy calls cherubs. The faces without the bodies had no wings and were called Ricky Martin and Kevin Fitzgerald.

"What are doing up there, ye eejits?" Úna demanded to know.

Kait looked up and asked softly, "Where's yer bodies?" For an answer, a pile of lumps of wool were thrown down on top of us. We ran screaming to the door of the warehouse with strands of wool clinging onto our heads and shoulders.

When we got near the door, the boys' aim wasn't good enough to hit us, which gave Úna and Ev a chance to organise and tell us what to do. Bunched together, we twisted our heads in different directions, surveying the battlefield. Turning around so we were face to face again, we each reported back on what we had observed and outlined our plans for a counterattack, like they do in the matinee pictures on Sunday.

Our enemy, Ricky Martin and Kevin Fitzgerald, were lying on the floor of the loft, which was the roof of the wool warehouse. There was a ladder going up to that part of the wool shed but it was in the line of fire. We would be exposed to enemy ammunition until we reached it. As I was the tallest, the other girls decided I would act as a shield and they crouched behind me. We ran from bale to bale and reached the ladder without being shot too often. As I climbed up, wool missiles rained down on me, making me look like a woolly snowman. I was protecting Úna and Evelyn who were right behind me. Kait was the last in line and shook with every step she took on every rung on the ladder.

Once we got into the attic, we rushed blindly at the boys and threw as much wool at them as they threw at us. In the middle of the battle, we heard Kait half crying, half screeching saying, "I can't let go of the ladder. I'm afraid to move." She was nearly on the last rung but was so frightened, she had frozen and couldn't move. The battle ceased. We all looked at poor Kait's white, terrified face.

A hand appeared out of nowhere and put itself on top of Kait's one. A nearly-grown-up voice told her to hold on to his two hands, he would make sure she didn't fall. Jim Smith had been there the whole time of the battle, lying on the loose wool that was spread out on the floor, smoking and not bothering with us kids until the damsel in distress needed help.

"What's wrong with you, cry baby?" Ricky Martin taunted but stopped when he saw the look on Jim's face. He quickly turned around towards where Evelyn was, pretending he was saying it to her. She shoved him and he shoved her back until Úna told them to stop.

"Hey, we are supposed to be getting boxes for Mr Ward and not acting the eejits with ye lads."

"Will we help ye?" the lads asked us.

Jim Smith said to Kait, "I'll go down the ladder in front of you. You don't have to be afraid of falling cos I'll hold you around the waist."

"I won't fall then, so I won't, if you are holding me." When she landed safely on the floor, Jim Smith helped wipe off the bits of wool that were stuck to her clothes. When Úna saw this, she remembered that Ducking Night Kait had found the ring in the barm breac and how Kait had said she wanted to marry Jim Smith.

"Kait, me and Arlene and Evelyn are going to carry a few boxes each to your uncle's house, so we don't need you," said Úna.

"I want to help too, so I do," she insisted as her hand fluttering like a butterfly on a flower as she waved it to say goodbye to Jim.

Ricky Martin ran behind Evelyn trying to push her, but she turned on him. She was the one who did the pushing even though she was only half his size. I saw Kevin Fitzgerald looking at me, but he didn't chance pushing me because maybe his sister Loretta had told him I would step on him like my daddy stamped on his cigarette butts. When we were at the door and nearly out, he called after me, "Arlene Daddy Long Legs."

Mrs Rushe, who was buying a sliced pan in Moran's shop, gave us awful looks as we raced past the shop shedding wool on the path. We had boxes on our heads, in our hands and in front of our feet that we were kicking along the street to Dun na Rí Road.

Mr Ward couldn't believe all the boxes we had managed to get him.

"Ye are great altogether, girls. If ye are around tomorrow, come up to the house and give us a hand."

"A course we will cos we know how to pack, so we do," Kait assured him, still flushed from her escapade on the ladder and her rescue by Jim Smith.

The next few days, we watched as Kait's uncle wrapped dish clothes and towels around the delph and placed the bundle into the crates. He put the statue of Martin De Porras, the picture of the Sacred Heart and a bottle of Knock holy water into the different folds of a blanket that he then put into a cardboard box. The bolster cases from the bed were packed tight with sheets and blankets and tied at the top with a string. Eithne was going to carry one of them under her arm and hold a suitcase in her hand. Shelia and Ciaran had to carry a pillowcase each packed with their boots and clothes.

The day before they left, Mr Ward boarded up the windows at the back of the house. He wasn't worried about the front ones because the neighbours would see if anyone went in through them.

He left the boxes and crates in the downstairs room, telling Nanny Ward that as soon as he had a few shillings put together, he'd get a van to pick them and bring them to the flat he had rented in London.

The next day, very early in the morning, the four of them left Drumbron. They went on the train to London while we were asleep in our beds.

The van never came for the boxes and crates. One day some lads were playing on the street outside Eithne's house. Without meaning to, one of the downstairs front windows got broken with a stone.

During the winter, we noticed the paint on the door was peeling. After Easter, it got worse. We were worried Mr Ward would be mad when he came home in the summer, but the Wards didn't come home on holiday.

A little while before we started fifth class, a family from Clonthu Hill left their caravan and started living in the Ward's house. It was strange to see them there and sad. Now we knew we might never again see Kait's cousins again or get an ice-cream cone from her uncle Martin in Jimmy Moran's shop.

In September, we went into fifth class. Our nun was called Sr Joseph. She had a normal face but didn't get cross with anyone, especially not with Loretta who still didn't know how to do multiplication tables off by heart. After the first few days, Sr Joseph never asked Loretta anything but every Friday, when we were going home, she stuck the paper-star on the little squirt's hand for being the best in the class.

We didn't care because fifth class was better than fourth, with lots of new things to do. It was hard for Loretta but easy for us and in the evenings, we were able to help Úna mind her old, new baby brother Francis Xavier in the pram and not have to do our lessons. The new baby, Aisling, stayed at home with the mammy.

Sometimes when we were pushing the pram around town, we saw Cathal McHugh drunk and falling all over the place. People used to say, "There goes poor Cathal, legless again." Mr Delaney didn't like him one bit and used to talk to Mammy about him and called him Legless instead of Cathal.

"That Legless McHugh is making an awful show of himself."

"And how's that, John?"

"There isn't a day that goes by he isn't legless, falling around the town and cursing the priests and bishop, saying he hopes they'll rot in hell for what they have done to him."

"How dare he talk like that about the bishop. I wonder does William know?"

"He must because Legless was throwing stones at the bishop's house again. The spell in Ballinacora didn't do him much good."

"There's more than him whose children have gone, and they don't go on like that."

Mrs McLoughlin was in the kitchen making me a sandwich. When she heard him talking, she got the brush and flew into the parlour and started sweeping around him and banging into the back of the armchair. Mammy looked at her surprised and said, "Mrs McLoughlin, I thought you were making Mary's tea."

"That girl is well able to make her own tea. Isn't she learning cookery at school?"

"Yes, Mammy, we have cookery class cos we are in fifth class," I said and tried not to laugh when I saw Mr Delaney had spilled some tea on his trousers with the banging Mrs McLoughlin had given the chair.

Classes

We started Cookery and Laundry Work with Sister Fursey. Twice a week, we made a line and went to the Domestic and Cookery room. It was a long room with a cooker and two sinks and a long white table but no chairs. We stood behind the table and looked at the nun at the top. She showed us what we had to do.

In laundry class, the nun put basins with water on the table and planks of wood with rugged surface, like a galvanised roof. She called the wavy planks washing boards. We put them into the water and rubbed rags and socks with a bar of soap on the boards, so as to wash them. It was great fun. We hung the clothes on a line in the class with pegs that were kept in a cloth bag. Sister Fursey showed us how to iron them with an electric iron like Mrs McLoughlin used in our house.

Ev said, "I haven't a notion of ever sticking my hands into that sudsy water. You don't see Sr Fursey getting Loretta and her friends to wash the auld dirty socks, do ya?"

Úna and Kait weren't interested either in the laundry class. They said they were tired of helping their mothers doing the washing at home in the tin tub. Mrs McLoughlin did our laundry and ironing, but I liked messing about with the water, so I didn't have any problems with the class.

Sr Fursey told us we needed white, starched aprons and caps for the cookery class. The apron was a wrap-around white skirt and had a big square in front for your chest with wide straps that went over the shoulders and crossed in an x and were buttoned into the thick waistband at the back. The cap was flounced at the back with elastic, so your hair could be tucked into it. A wide band like the peak on a cap was sewed into the front and covered the hair in front and the forehead. Ev called it a maid's outfit. Mammy bought my cookery class things in the drapery shop where the man with the eyes bulging out of his head eyes looked at her and other women. Sr Fursey made Úna and Kait ashamed because their mammies had no money to buy the aprons. The nun stood in front of the class and said, "I know there are girls in this class who are too poor to buy the clothes for the cookery class, so I will let them use some old aprons that I keep in this press for this purpose." She unlocked a press and called Úna, Kait and some other girls up and handed them an apron.

The first day at cookery class, Sr Fursey said we had to be in a team of ten. She told Loretta to pick her team and they went to the table near the nun's small one. The four of us, with Fionnuala McCabe, Pauline Byrne and Colette Day plus three more girls, stood together at the same table and watched as Sr Fursey showed us how to cream butter and sugar together in a yellow bowl with a wooden spoon.

At our table, I was the first to be start mixing the two ingredients together. The cold, solid butter and the sugar didn't blend into each other easily. However, when Sr Fursey told Úna to take the bowl from me and beat the mixture, the two ingredients came together like grainy sand for her. With Ev the grains got smaller and when Kait took the bowl, it had started to get creamy. The next few girls in our team kept beating until what was in the bowl became loose and fluffy. When the eggs were added it looked like golden milk. After the flour was sieved into the bowl, we all took turns beating the mixture until it was light and airy.

While we waited for the nun to come and see what we had done, we looked over at Loretta's table. She had only stirred her mixture around for a second and whined her arm was tired. The nun told her to stop and gave Noeleen and Regina Burke extra time beating the mixture in the bowl. The nun let us grease the two baking tins but wouldn't let us pour the runny stuff into them or put the tins into the oven. She did that part herself. While the cakes were baking, we washed up the bowl and spoon and swept the flour. Loretta didn't do anything because she needed to rest.

When the four half cakes came out of the oven, Sr Fursey told Loretta to spread jam on the two bottom sides and put the thick round slices together like a sandwich. The nun called the yellow-beige-y cake a Victoria Sponge. She gave one whole cake for Loretta to take home. She cut the other cake into wedges and we all got a paper-thin slice to eat.

On other days we made drop scones, rock buns, scones, soda bread and piles of lovely things. At home, I told Mrs McLoughlin what I had learned, and she let me make cakes in the kitchen. Ev said she wasn't interested in learning to bake because she could buy her cakes in Wynn's if she felt like eating something sweet. We learned how to make dinners too, like shepherd's pie and the stuffing for a chicken and other types of dinners. The four of us thought the nun ruined the lovely dinner of boiled bacon and cabbage by pouring parsley sauce over it.

After cookery-class day, when I brought my apron and cap home to wash, Mammy said she would send it to the Magdalene Laundry as Mrs McLoughlin wouldn't have time to starch it. A wagon-type cart from the Magdalene Laundry used to call to pick up our bed linen, as Mammy called the sheets and pillowcases. Mrs McLoughlin did our normal washing, but the sheets were difficult to dry and ironed, so they were sent to the laundry in Galway to get them washed and starched.

I was the best in the class at drawing, even though Fionnuala McCabe was good too and so was Colette Daly. Singing class was smashing with the nun hitting the tuning-fork to see what type of voices we had and where to put us in the choir according to how high we sang. In sewing class, we learned how to sew and darn. Mammy said no one darned socks anymore. It made me think of the Home Babies and the jumpers they wore that were made of the ripped-out different socks the nun couldn't darn anymore.

I wondered if Liam was still wearing a many-lined *geansaí* with puckered up sleeves, like he used to wear in first class.

I loved history. It was just like listening to Daddy tell me stories about places and people. There was a time Ireland was full of Saints and Scholars. The scholars were monks who wrote the bible and Irish stories on manuscripts that were made of leather. There were copy-cats in the monasteries who copied other monk's writing and caused wars when they were found out, like St Colmcille. He copied a whole book and when the king told him to give the copy back to the monk saying, "To every cow its calf. To every book its copy." Colmcille fought to keep the manuscript. There were more than 3,000 people killed and the copycat monk went off to Iona and became a saint.

After the saints and scholars, the Vikings came. First, they attacked the monks who ran into the High Towers with their treasures but then they stopped doing that. Instead of attaching the Irish people, they married them and learned the Irish language and built towns. Everything was fine until Diarmuid MacMurrough messed things up. Diarmuid and Tiernan O'Rourke fought and Diarmuid was driven out of Ireland. He went to England and brought Strongbow and the Danes back with him to fight O'Rourke and get his lands back. After that, the English started coming and instead of learning Irish they forced us to speak English. Some of the English Kings were cruel and Queen Elizabeth was very cruel. She used tar-caps and put them on people's heads. Cromwell was terrible, the worst of all. I hope he is burning in hell forever and doesn't know the act of contrition, so he is not saved from fires, because he made the Irish people suffer too much.

"Daddy, why were the English so cruel to us? Why did they hate us?"

"They didn't hate the people, they just thought the Irish were savages."

"That's stupid, we weren't savages."

"The English saw the people here in Ireland wearing different clothes and the men with long hair, they didn't know what to make of them. It must have frightened them."

"A pity about them. It still didn't give them any right to kill us or put tar-caps on us or make us stop speaking our own language."

"Things were different then. The English wanted to civilise the Irish and teach them a better way of life."

"We were civilised with our own Brehon laws and our High Kings. We didn't need them to teach us anything."

"Ach, lass, they didn't see it like that. Are you learning as much geography as you are learning history?" he asked so I would stop talking about what the English had done.

"I am but I don't know where the Yellow Ford is."

"Why do you want to know where it is?"

"Cos I like Shane O'Neill. I called my guardian angel Shane. It sounds lovely, nicer than Seán. Daddy, when you have time will you bring me to where the Battle of the Yellow Ford was?"

"Imagine a wee one like you wanting to know about battlefields. Do I have a little rebel on my hands?"

"I amn't a rebel, Daddy. I just want to know. If you don't want to bring me there, you could show me the place on the mountain where they found Red Hugh O'Neill in the snow, after he escaped from the prison in Dublin."

"We'll see, pet."

'We'll see' meant 'No' so we'd never go to see the mountain where Red Hugh O'Neill was. At least I saw Mr Ward, Eithne and their children the summer Maura McLoughlin did her Inter Cert.

It was around Easter time when Úna told us her cousins from Liverpool were coming to stay in her house and she wondered what they would think of her brother's farts.

"Will we go to the station and meet them coming off the train?" we asked all excited.

"What good would it do? First, I don't know what they look like and second, we never let them into our show free, so their daddy wouldn't buy us an ice-cream in Jimmy Moran's like Mr Ward used to do," Úna explained.

"What bed are they going to sleep in?" Kait wanted to know.

"Ya, where will ye put them, Úna?" I wondered because there were so many already in Úna's house.

"Mammy says we'll put a mattress on the floor for the children."

"And the mother and father?" I asked.

"They'll go into Mammy and Daddy's bed."

"The four big people together in one bed?" Evelyn asked surprised.

"No silly goose, Mam and Dad go into our bed, Bernie's and mine, and we go in with my small brothers in their bed."

"But there's still no room for four people in a bed," I said. "How will ye fit?"

"There is so! Two of us will sleep at the top and two at the bottom."

"We do the same when our relatives come," Kait told us. "The visitors get Mammy and Daddy's bed in the front room. We all pile up in the back room. I hate it cos my brother has worms, and they make him twist and turn all night and Mary sticks her feet into my face."

"My brother Brendan farts, and the smell is awful," Úna reminded us.

Listening to my friends laughing about having their sister's toe stuck in their mouths and having to share the bed with three others, I didn't say our house was big because it might sound like boasting, so I said, "Smelling your brothers' farts might be better than smelling Mr Delaney's coffee."

"Oh, that delicious aroma of Italian coffee," Ev said mocking Mr Delaney's way of talking because we didn't like him, but when Úna's big cousin, Ann, came and spoke different from us, we didn't mock her because we liked her. We spent the week she was on holidays asking her about

Liverpool and if she had ever seen the Beatles when she was out playing. She hadn't but she told us all the girls in Liverpool wore short skirts and dresses above their knees and long cardigans like she did, and they didn't dress old-fashioned, like we did.

"And are there eejits in Liverpool like those two?" Ev said pointing to Ricky Martin and Kevin Fitzgerald who were always following Ann around everywhere on their bikes, even up to Clonthu Hill to Nan Gormley's.

Nan was Ann's grandmother and the English girl wanted to be with her 'Gran' all the time. It was hard to get her to go anywhere except Clonthu but once we managed to get her back to river where Kevin, Seán, Tom and Mel McNally were fishing with a line, hook and cork. The lads acted stupid telling Ann they were big and boasting they had done their Primary Cert. They were sorta mocking us saying we were in a lower class than them and only going into sixth class and still had another year to do before we finished primary school. Ev got fed up with them and said that as least our voices didn't croak and go squeaky like theirs did.

When Ann and her family were leaving, we went to the station with Úna to say goodbye and were sad for a while without her, but then, two weeks before Sports Day, Kait told us her uncle, Mr Ward, Eithne and her cousins Shelia and Ciaran were coming to stay in her house. We wanted to go to the station to meet them, but we couldn't because it was the same day as Sport's Day, and we were in Castle Fields when they arrived.

The next day we met Kait in Kilmartin Road. She was complaining about her cousin.

"Shelia is a silly goose."

"Why?"

"Well, the first thing she said to me was, 'Are you Oirish?' And I said to her, 'No, I'm Kait.' She didn't know who I was, so she didn't."

Shelia had a funny way of talking from the roof of her mouth and asking us, 'Ave you been ove' 'ere long?' After a few days running around Kilmartin Road, Shelia began to sound a bit more like us. Sheila's father, Mr Ward, wanted Nanny to go and live with him in London and told her to give away her furniture.

"*A cailíní*, it is hard to be old and going to a land that is strange."

"Nanny, why don't you stay here and not go to London with Uncle Martin?"

"Marteen thinks he's doing the right thing taking me to live with him. He's wanting to mind me like I minded him when his father died and him only a garsoon."

We didn't want Nanny to leave and take all her *piseogs* and stories about the fairies and the Black and Tans with her, as well as her clay pipe and snuff. Nan Gormley wasn't going away but she said a *brónach mór* was on her on account of Molly going away. She told us not to torment her for a while as her heart was heavy and weighing her body down but come and see Nanny as much as we could while she was still in her house on Clonthu Hill.

Mammy didn't know where I went. If she had known, she'd have had a fit, because she didn't like people from council-houses. Herself and her coffee friends were always tutting about how country girls and the ones from council houses were getting notions, thinking they were too good to work as servant girls. Mammy seemed to forget our daily help, as she called Mrs McLoughlin, lived in a council house on Kilmartin Road. She came every day, except Saturday and Sunday, chatting to Mammy, telling her how she had finished the ironing and was going clean the windows or hoover the stairs.

At least Mammy spoke to Mrs McLoughlin when we saw her uptown or at Mass, but she didn't salute my friends' mothers, only Mrs Curry. Mrs Curry was Ev's mammy who came to our house for elevenses with the others from the golf course and the bridge club. Evelyn's mother was such a special friend of Mammy's that Mr Delaney promised he'd get her a coffee percolator the next time he went to Rome. He also helped Mrs Curry choose the new carpets and curtains for her house.

Ev said Mr Delaney gave her the creeps. "He's an eejit, talking about how an orangey-yellow would be ideal for the tiles in the bathroom. When I said it would match the shite that goes down the toilet, Mammy got cross."

"Did you say that? Mammy would have a fit if I said that to Mr Delaney."

"She only told me not to be annoying them and to go out to play or she'd tell Daddy I was bold when he got home."

Evelyn was a bit of a devil. She loved doing bold, tomboy things like jumping over ditches, walking on high walls, playing rough stuff with the football, robbing apples from the trees, swimming in the river, talking to the tinkers in their caravans or going up to Nanny's house to sit beside the fire, drinking tea out of the tin mug and smoking the clay pipe or putting snuff up her nose.

Our mothers knew we were the best of friends, so while they knew Evelyn was with me and I was with her, we had no problem and we could spend all the time up on Clonthu Hill, telling Nanny not to worry about Mick the Sticks. When the man with only one leg had no money to pay for a night's lodgings, Nanny let him sleep in her kitchen. Now, that she was going to London, she wondered where he would spend the night when he had no money, and worried that Jack the Lantern would trick Mick into following him and his light through the countryside.

"*A cailíní*, be sure and let Mick the Sticks know my door is on the latch and he is free to sleep here any night he wants."

"Why Nanny, do you want him to mind it for you?"

"I don't but his one leg is tired of carrying the weight of his body. If that cunning little weasel with the lantern is around, when Mick hasn't the money for a night's lodging, he'll trick the poor man into following him."

"Who is the weasel with the lantern?"

"Jack the Lantern."

"What does he do, Nanny?"

"In the darkness of night when a wanderer sees the light from Jack's lantern, they think there is a house nearby, and head in that direction."

"Why do they want to talk to Jack?"

"No, *a storín beag*, they'd be looking for somewhere to sleep after tramping the road the whole day long."

"But the people of the house mightn't let them in."

"*A mhuirnín*, the ones who walk the roads know that. There'd be no fear of them knocking on the farmhouse door. What they want is any kind of shelter with a bit of a roof to keep them dry for the night."

"Why don't you want Mick following Jack the Lantern?"

"The villain would lead the poor creature along boreens, over ditches and into fields and bogs until he dropped dead from weariness and tiredness the way the tramps do when they follow his light."

Sometimes me and my pals saw tramps around town, but we didn't know they had no houses to sleep in. One day a beggar knocked on our door. Mammy opened it and then half closed it. The man looked like Robert Taylor from the matinee pictures, only his hair was falling down on his forehead in curly waves. Mammy spoke to him through the gap that wasn't closed.

"Mistress, there wouldn't be any jobs you need doing around house or yard?"

"My husband takes care of everything. There is no work for you, so be off."

"Mistress, I'm cheap paid. At the end of the day, I only ask for a bite to eat or any auld clothes your husband mightn't be needing." Mammy closed the door on his face and told Daddy about him. "William, I think something should be done about the tramps who go knocking on people's doors. I can assure you they are up to no good."

"Dervla, most of them are harmless. They are from the industrial schools. When they leave, they have nowhere to go."

"I don't care where he was before he came to my door. William, he frightened me out of my wits."

"Don't be worrying. They won't do you any harm. The Brothers knocked any spunk they had out of them."

She kept on but Daddy said he had to go to the pitch and left again. When Mr Delaney called around, she told him about how the man had smelled. "I'd say he hadn't washed in days."

"Don't be talking to me about them tramps. Only last week, one called to my mother's house but thank God I was out the back and able to stop him from annoying Mother."

"Was he looking for money too?"

"He was but before I gave him any, I made him go into the outhouse and strip off and have a wash for himself."

"Weren't you good, John."

"He was only a young fellow and I had to show him how to wash his body."

"He didn't know how to wash himself?"

"I'd say he was out of an industrial school, so I made sure he washed behind his ears and wherever else that needed washing."

"Wasn't that very good of you."

"I told him if he behaved, I'd give him some clothes and a few bob."

"I hope he was grateful."

"The looks he gave me were not to my liking. He didn't want what I had for him, but he took it in the end."

"We could do with more like you in this town."

"Dervla, to put your mind at ease, I'll drive around to find that fellow and to tell him a thing or two about frightening decent women." Before he left, he gave Mammy the latest news. "That Legless is a case onto himself. But leaving that aside, did you hear the Wards are taking the grandmother to London with them?"

"Sure, with the way things are going there'll be very few families left in Kilmartin Road at all. All running for the boat and the easy life in England instead of staying in their own country and working."

"That England is a pagan place. They have strikes every second day of the week and no respect for the family. At the same time, it good it's there for the ones we don't want here."

"How's that John?"

"Well, my father said that W T Cosgrove thought emigration was good to rid the country of the children born in workhouses."

"My father had great respect for W T Cosgrove. What was it that he said?"

"Ah something about them who want to live at the expense of the ratepayers being better abroad, because they will have to work whether they like it or not."

"He was right, John, but there will always be people who don't want to work. They are the very first ones to head off when they think they'll have it easy in England. I heard Mrs Fitzgerald saying at the golf course it is next to impossible to get a servant girl who willing to work the hours that are needed to keep a house clean and tidy."

While they were complaining I slipped out and went up Clonthu Hill where Úna and the pram were. Evelyn was sitting by the hob, smoking Nanny's clay pipe. Kait came five minutes later.

"Are you coming up the Sandy Hills with us?" Ev asked her.

"A course. When are we going?"

"Not until it gets dark."

"What are you waiting for it to get dark?"

"To catch Jack the Lantern and make him promise not to lead Mick the Sticks over the hills and into a ditch," Ev told us.

"Great but first I have something to tell Nanny about Mick the Sticks, so she's not worried," Kait said so we went with her to where Nanny was sitting.

"Nanny, don't be worrying about Mick The Sticks. He can become a pirate like Long John Silver."

"Who's that Long John, a girleen?"

"He has a parrot on his shoulder that squawks and a black patch on his eyes and he is one-legged like Mick the Sticks."

"I never heard tell of him, *a stóir*. Where would he be living now?"

"Nanny, he lives in his ship."

"On the Suileen River?"

"We saw him in the Odeon on Sunday."

"Why would they let a man like that with only one leg into the Odeon?"

"Nanny, he was in the picture."

"What picture?"

"The one we went to at the matinee, and we saw the parrot on his shoulder, so we did," Kait said.

"Devil the fear of Mick having a bird on his shoulder, more like him having it in the pot and a few spuds boiling alongside it. It's not often the poor man gets a good feed."

"But Nanny if Mick had a sword, he could fight Jack the Lantern."

"Is it in Ballinacora ye want him locked up in? If the Gardaí saw Mick waving a knife about, they'd say his mind was gone with the drink and have the judge sign him into the madhouse."

We saw she didn't understand, so the gang of us started walking towards the Sand Hills, taking turns pushing the pram that rocked from side to side and made a squeaky noise. It was hard to push it. Francis Xavier and the other baby were getting cranky as could be, but we knew we had to save Mick the Sticks from Jack the Lantern.

"Why don't you go home, Úna. The babies are sleepy," Ev told her.

"I don't want to," she said, so we continued even though we were beginning to have doubts about the hunt.

Just outside town, Ricky Martin, Kevin Fitzgerald and Jim Smith whizzed by on their bikes. We were pushed into the side of the road as they passed by.

Úna called after them, "Do ye want us to end up in the ditch or what, ye eejits?"

"Where are ye going without a bell on yer bikes?" Evelyn roared after them.

We laughed because everyone knew the joke about the Gardaí stopping people and asking them, 'And now where would you be going without a bell on your bike?'

They had gone on a bit but turned around and swung back towards us. Ricky Martin came whizzing to a stop in front of Evelyn, who was pushing the pram.

"What are ya doing pushing with that filthy, old thing that looks like a bathtub?"

"It's not a bathtub, ya blind bat."

"I know it isn't, cos you wash in a bath and them two filthy kids haven't seen a lick of soap or water for ages."

"How dare you call my brothers kids! They are children. My mother isn't a goat, you jackass," Úna shouted at him. At school, the nuns told us we shouldn't use kids for children because it was an American expression. In Ireland, everyone knew kids meant baby goats.

"I wasn't talking to you, Gingernut. I was talking to her," he said looking at Evelyn.

Instead of answering him Evelyn pushed him off the bike and said, "I'll break your neck if ya open your mouth again to say anything bad about Úna's pram or about the children."

Jim Smith had got his bike and was looking at Kait and telling her, "Me and the lads are going to Brown's field to get some apples. Will I bring you back a few?"

"The farmer might see ya, so he might, and tell the Gardaí."

"I don't care if he does. The apples are lovely and sweet, so I'll get you a big juicy one."

The news about the apples was just what we needed to change our plans, so we decided to go to Brown's field with the boys. They stayed on their bikes, walking more than cycling. Kevin Fitzgerald stayed near me, but I pretended I didn't see him. When it was Kait's turn to push the pram, Jim Smith said he'd do it for her. Evelyn got on his bike and started racing with Ricky Martin, shouting back at him, "Hurry up, slowcoach, I'm tired waiting for you to catch up."

"You're only winning me cos Jim's bike is better than mine."

When we got near Brown's field, we saw the farmer driving his cows up the lane, so we turned around and headed back to town with the lads. We told them we were going to see Robin Hood in the Odeon on Sunday. They said they'd see us there before they sped off on their bikes.

That night in bed I was wondering did the English nannas wear long skirts and shawls like Nanny Ward did. I hope they did, otherwise people would be looking at her thinking she was odd because she didn't wear a coat. The next day we headed up to her house. Inside I was crying when I grabbed her around her skirt and hugged her legs real tight, but I kept the tears in, because I saw Nan Gormley, who would miss her more than us, change her sad face into a happy one when she came to say goodbye.

"Molly, *tráth*, we'll never feel it until you are back to us telling us how the people in London live."

The Boat to England

Nanny and the Wards left for England. We never saw her again and she never saw Úna McNulty's new baby sister, Eimear and wasn't around to say 'God bless you' to protect Eimear from the fairies taking her and leaving a changeling in her place. She wouldn't know that at end of sixth class, Úna's daddy found another baby under a head of cabbage and that after a while Baby Patrick was put in the pram with Eimear. She wasn't standing at the door looking at us pushing the pram with the wobbly wheels up the hill to her house. Nanny would never see the new pram the McNulty's were thinking of buying if their father got a job in the new factory.

Everyone was talking about the new factory that was after opening near the Suileen river. Mr Delaney knew about the factory long before it was built and told Daddy and Dr Kelly to buy land around the area where the factory was going to be. He said when it was re-zoned, they would be able to build houses and make a bit of money for themselves. Úna's family and others on her road were hoping there would be work for them, that way there'd be no need for them to go to England, like Maura McLoughlin was going to do.

"Dervla, is that another one of them young hussies off to England to get rid of her sin?" Mr Delaney said between stuffing lumps of Chester cake into his mouth.

"John, how could think that of Maura?" Mammy said in one of the few times she ever disagreed with him. "Her mother has brought her up to a good girl and she did very well in her Inter Cert. That is why she is off to work with the nuns in Liverpool."

Maura McLoughlin and the five Honours she got in her Inter Cert exam was the talk of the town.

"That girl is a credit to you, Mrs McLoughlin," Mammy said to Maura's mother while she was ironing one of Daddy's shirts.

"Indeed, she is a great girl. Never gave me a bit of trouble."

"It's not many the girl who can boast of getting five Honours in their Inter Cert."

"That's true and the poor girleen working in Wynn's after school and not being able to go up to the convent for study time like her friends."

"I didn't know there was study time in the convent."

"It starts at five and finishes at seven o'clock when the boarders go for their supper. Near the exams they go from eight to nine too."

"A good way to have the girls study."

"It is but still and all, Maura managed to get five Honours without going."

"I saw she was a smart girl when used to come here."

"That she is. I'll miss her when she goes off to Liverpool next month."

"And you were saying the reason she is going is what again?"

"As she's gone sixteen, she wants to leave school and start working. I went to Fr Mannion to see if he knew of anything going."

"Did he help you?"

"Oh, he was of great help. He told us about a nursing order of nuns in Liverpool. It seems they take in young Irish girls to work in their hospital and when the girls turn eighteen, they go on to become student nurses."

"Isn't that great altogether. Maura will become a nurse."

"It will take a few years before she is qualified."

"Where will she be staying in Liverpool?"

"The nuns take care of that. They have a nurse's residence, so she doesn't have to look for anywhere to stay."

"That's a great worry off your mind, knowing the nuns are there to keep an eye on her."

"Indeed, it is, and on top of all that she'll be getting paid and be able to send me a few bob every week."

"Isn't that great, now. Mary and I are off downtown. What would you think would be a good farewell present for Maura."

"There's no need to buy her anything, Mrs Blake."

"But we couldn't let her leave without giving her a little something."

"That's very good of you. The truth is in the letter they sent, the nursing nuns said she needs two nightdresses with her name sewn on the back, so maybe if a nightdress isn't too much, that would be great."

"I'll get her two."

"Not at all Mrs Blake, one will be fine, sure she has the one she made in the Domestic Science class with Sister Fursey. And the Wynn's were so good as to get her a pair of slippers, a twin set and gloves."

The morning Maura left, her mother helped her carry her suitcase down to station, from where she would get the train to the boat. Mrs McLoughlin went with her as far as Drumbeag, the first stop on the train.

At Drumbeag, before Mrs McLoughlin got off the train, she looked at her sixteen-year-old daughter who had never left Drumbron in her life and said, "Now a girleen, there isn't much I can say to you except to remember to say your prayers and be a good girl."

"A course I will, Mammy but where will I get the boat. Will it say Liverpool on it?"

"Follow the crowd, Maura *a grá*. Look at the ones who have a suitcase because they'll be getting on the boat, too."

"But Mammy, they all won't be going to Liverpool."

"Well, a girl, they'll be going to England and then you ask, and you'll get to where you are going."

Mrs McLoughlin hugged Maura and got off the train before her daughter saw the pool of water glimmering at the bottom of her eyes. She stood on the platform as the train pulled out, waving to Maura, who had her face pressed against the windowpane. Then she walked back to Drumbron as she didn't have the money for the ticket for the train fare back.

That evening when she came to our house to tidy it up, her feet were swollen. I asked her what had happened. In a jerky voice that cracked and stopped as she swallowed spits, she told me how she had gone with her little girl and given her the only advice she had. On the long walk back, she prayed every prayer she knew asking God to mind her child. I wondered if Mammy had known Mrs McLoughlin had to carry the suitcase to the station and walk back from Drumbeag, would she have given them a lift instead of going to the golf course?

Maura left in 1965 after we finished fifth class. In September, we started sixth class with Sr Bosco. It was the last year of primary school and things were the same as always.

There was going to be another baby to take the place of the last one in the pram because after the summer, Úna's mammy was going to get another baby. Úna had nine McNulty's in her family and I only had one Blake – me. I asked Daddy to sow cabbages in our back garden, but he said he was too busy at the pitch with the GAA.

Mammy was listening and said, "The pitch, is it? The one with the music and dancing and queer going on?" meaning the dance hall in the parish hall, where the old people went to dance waltzes and quick steps. Mr Delaney and Mammy didn't like it, saying it was worse than Sodom and Gomorrah and if they didn't watch out, God would destroy it with fire and brimstone. I knew it wasn't true because Daddy helped Fr Mannion and Miss Walsh from the library organise the dances. If God was going to do anything to the hall, Daddy would know cos he was a Garda, and the Gardaí knew everything.

At the end of sixth Class, we did our Primary Cert. Our nun, Sr Bosco, told us it was to test our Irish, English and Arithmetic so we could obtain a certificate to say we had finished primary school. We sat at our desks and our nun, Sr Bosco, placed a paper with the exam written on it in front of us. Loretta started crying. She said she couldn't answer the questions. Sr Bosco told Regina and Noeleen to help her and tell her what to write. Even then she still couldn't do it, so Sr Bosco went down to her desk and showed her what to write. It was dead easy for me and my pals. We finished it really quickly because we knew after the exam, we had holidays and we wanted to get out the door as quick as we could, not realising it was our last day in primary school and we would never go back again.

After summer, me and my pals would be going to secondary school. Daddy showed me the old building on Church Street with the high, grey wall with the spiky glass on top and the thick solid, iron door to go in through, I asked him why the secondary school was such a small, dark, dreary building and not nice and bright like the primary school on Cork Road. He explained to me that during the

Penal Laws, when it was against the law for Irish children to go to school, the sons and daughters of the wealthy Irish Catholic families were sent to boarding schools and convents on the Continent to be educated. The poorer children went to Hedge Schools.

When the Penal Laws disappeared, a Drumbron merchant petitioned a French order of nuns to come to Ireland to educate the young ladies of the town. He gifted the nuns two small buildings in Church Street. They used one as their dwelling place and the other as the school. At the beginning, there was only the small convent school for all the girls of the town. Daddy said that after the War of Independence, things improved in Ireland and the government built primary schools all over the country and gave them to nuns to teach the children in.

Our primary school was lovely with the statue of Our Lady outside in the green garden and the grainy-white walls with the bright, lacy, see-through railings and the wide gate that opened in two, and where you could fit your foot in the gaps and swing on it. When we skipped out onto Cork Street, at the end of June, it never crossed our minds it would be the last time we would be using the gate.

Lots of girls would not be coming back in September. They would be leaving forever the school we had been in since Low Babies. When I asked Mammy why, she told me secondary school wasn't free like primary school and not everyone could afford it.

"Will they stay at home and be out all day playing?"

"I doubt it, if they are lucky, they'll start working in houses around Drumbron and if not, they will go to England."

"Like Maura McLoughlin on the boat?"

"They will go on the boat but not to a good job like Maura."

"Does that mean we will only have a few girls in our class in first year?" I asked her as I saw she was talking to me, which she did seldom, and I wanted to find out as much as possible about the new school.

"The class will be full."

"How can it be full if half the girls won't be there?"

"Because the nuns have a boarding school. Girls from all over the country will be coming to study in Drumbron."

"That's funny cos some of the girls in our class are going as boarders to other schools and other girls are coming as boarders to our school."

"I know, by right you should go to the same school as Loretta Fitzgerald, but your father won't hear of it."

I knew well Mammy wanted me to be a boarder at the same school as Loretta, Regina and Noeleen but Daddy wanted me at home. I heard them fighting day after day about where I would study.

"Dervla, you can give out all you like but Arlene is staying at school here in Drumbron."

"William, this is her chance to mix with the right sort. Only the big people go to boarding school."

"I was sent to one of the best colleges, Pretoria in Enniskillen, but it wasn't home. I want Arlene here with us."

"William, she will be with for the holidays."

"Arlene is not going away to boarding school. We are lucky there is a secondary school in the town. If it is any way as good as the primary school, she will do well," he said using his Garda voice.

When Mammy told me I should be going to the same school as Loretta, Noeleen and Regina, I made the mistake of saying, "I'm glad I'm not going. I want to stay at home." Mammy's face started to change, and the vexed look was coming onto it, so I edged my way towards the door and headed off to find my friends who were waiting for me.

We knew that in September we would be going in through the gate on Church Street to the old building where the French nuns established their first school, but until then, we were free to enjoy summer.

Glossary of Terms

A grá	darling
A tráth	It's time/Indeed
Mhuirnín	darling
Smacht	manners/discipline
Daoine sibhe	fairy folk
A mhac ban	My fair son/my blonde boy
A mhic	son
a stóirín	sweetheart
Le cuige Dé	with the help of God
A grá me chroí	love of my heart
Banshee	ghost signalling a death
Coster Bower	headless coachman that collected souls
	Ná bé ag caint, tá na clasaí mór ar na páistí agus beal na more ar guid. Be quiet and don't be talking about what you hear.
a leanbh	child

leanaí	children
brónach	sadness
meas	respect
mar dhea	pretend
geansaí	jumper
cailíní	girls
piseog	superstition
peata	pet
duais	treat
Anseo	present/here
griog	tease
a cailín óg	small girl
dearóg	little fish
Día ar sábhául	God save
In ainm Dé!	In the name of God!
Oíche Samhain	Halloween
A rua	My red-haired one
A cratur	A creature
A stóirín beag	little sweetheart
Fadó	long ago
cailín dubh	bold girl
Mhaith an cailín	good girl
púca	ghost

binóg	scarf/wrap
Diabhail imhuid	damn it
Ba cheart é a chur soir	It should be placed east
haon, dó, trí	one, two, three
ceathar, cúig	four, five
cailín dána	bold girl
seordán	A piercing wind that screeches
óinseach	fool
rámhaille	rambling
spraoi	fun
Ná béid ag caint	Don't talk
Amadán	fool
sleán	tool for cutting turf, similar to a rectangular spade
Tigín agus rudí go leor	a little house and all the things
iar cul an tig	inside it
bata fada	long stick
buille	to hit, or a childhood game
bata beag	small stick
pucaí mushrooms	magic mushrooms
barm breac	sweet cake served with butter at Halloween

Coming Soon

The Figure in the Graveyard

The story continues with Arlene Blake and her friends as teenagers with all the typical teenage problems and insecurities growing up in 1970s Ireland. It was a time where 'The Troubles' were raging in the north of Ireland, emigration was rife and girls were hurriedly sent to their aunts in England to hide unwanted pregnancies. Set in an era where to be unwed and pregnant was morally shunned and shame and disgrace brought to the families door. Hence the need for quick action to make the problem disappear from ever seeing judging eyes and prejudice.

To her detriment, Arlene learns how oppressive grief and guilt can be used as forms of control, while the crying of the Ghost Babies of the restrained mothers, in the deserted grounds of the abandoned Home, are hushed into silence with a Mass and the sprinkling of Holy water.

Please Review

Dear Reader,

If you enjoyed this book, would you kindly post a short review on Amazon or Goodreads? Your feedback will make all the difference to getting the word out about this book.

To leave a review, go to Amazon and type in the book title. When you have found it and go to the book page, please scroll to the bottom of the page to where it says 'Write a Review' and then submit your review. Thank you in advance. Honor Harlow is a woman who thought she was going to live peacefully and quietly in her hometown among the people she knew. Life came along and took her elsewhere. The road she found herself on was bumpy and scary, and sometimes lonely. Against all odds, she kept going, seeing things that changed her. Now she writes what she has witnessed and experienced.

About the Author

Honor Harlow is a woman who thought she was going to live peacefully and quietly in her hometown among the people she knew. Life came along and took her elsewhere. The road she found herself on was bumpy and scary, and sometimes lonely. Against all odds, she kept going, seeing things that changed her. Now she writes what she has witnessed and experienced.

www.ingramcontent.com/pod-product-compliance
Lightning Source LLC
Chambersburg PA
CBHW021429080526
44588CB00009B/475